A WARRIOR'S LIFE

The life of Arnold Bondley, a Vietnam veteran
battling the PTSD minefield, fighting the war within

KAREN BONDLEY

Published by Karen Bondley

Written by Karen Bondley
Contributions by Allan McMurtry
Journal entries by Arnold Bondley

ISBN: 979-8-218-87241-0 (paperback)
First edition 2026

For book orders and enquiries, contact:
abondley@charter.net

This book is a work of nonfiction. However, some names have been changed to protect soldiers' identities.

"On Point" by Robert Jost reprinted from
Veterans of War, Veterans of Peace
with permission from Chiron Publications,
Asheville, North Carolina.

**Dedicated to all Vietnam veterans,
their families and friends**

A Warrior's Life is true account of how fate takes hold of our
lives and drives us to places we never wanted to go.

Acknowledgments

I want to thank my friends and family for supporting me in this
endeavor, especially Allan McMurtry who was in Vietnam with
my husband Arnold. His insights helped me to understand their
war and how it affected them when they returned home.

CONTENTS

FOREWORD

There will be wars and rumors of wars. Vietnam was not a rumor. Roughly 2.5 million mostly men served in Vietnam and Arnold was there at the peak contingent of some 550,000. He arrived by ship crawling north up the coast of Vietnam shortly after the 1968 Tet Offensive, landing in Da Nang, headquarters of I Corps, and served there with the 1st Marine Division until November 1969. As a VA doctor noted to me, "In IV Corps the 1968 Tet offensive lasted a few months, in I Corps it never stopped."

It isn't always how you spent your time in a war zone, sometimes it's just the raw amount of it in years, months, days, and seconds. Arnold saw his share of war at 19-20 years of age. It's a gallon of water in a one-quart jar. When you think you've had enough there is more. Some of 7th Psyops died in helicopters, some on the ground, some by mortar, some by others means. There were wounds to be treated and wounds unseen.

Tim O'Brien's short stories, *The Things They Carried,* noted the Army names for so many items of Vietnam combat, but there was no name for moral and ethical wounds. At the time there was "shell shock", "battle fatigue," and "Vietnam syndrome."

The most appropriate and telling might have been "soldier's heart" from the Civil War. All things being equal, nobody wanted to describe war, it was Civil or World or Liberation or Independence or some country. For the "soldier's heart" there was no salve, no tonic, no sutures or compressions. There was no handicap sticker or purple heart. Often there was no welcome home other than the sign at the special mess hall at Travis Air Force Base saying "welcome home and well done." Offering unlimited steak, French fries, and Cokes, it was unclear what well done they were talking about – the sirloin or the men walking in. All you could eat off metal tables, metal chairs, linoleum floors, and bright lights staring at white walls. Nobody stayed long, and the steak went cold quickly.

Arnold's welcome was the same. What family knew what to do or say? What company did? Even the VA didn't have funds or know how on what to do back then. Agent Orange could have been a cold drink, and that it could kill was a closely held secret. That it could extend to second, third, and maybe fifth generations was a lot of marriages in the future.

For Arnold, the solder's heart beat on through a singularly wonderful marriage, an architectural degree, a job with the City of Portland, and then the refuge of a seaside town and private practice in Oregon. He and Karen did well. But somewhere south of forgetting, things went wrong. The remaining three quarts of memories showed up and ran down the military commendations, the Bronze Star, the end of his architectural career, and a conscience that already had too much to carry. They finally ran him down. Though he died too early, his memory still lights the halls he walked, still springs to life among old friends, and remains welcome among the many people he befriended and helped.

Arnold is not alone. He is in a cemetery of heroes in the Willamette National Cemetery, in photos, and in memories of those who served with him.

Allan E. McMurtry, Sgt acting jack
7th Psyops detached, 1st Marine Division

On Point

He walks
Out of a Village Gate at Night
Past bunkers, looks
Out on the narrow road
And sees the possibility
Of death. And he doesn't care.
For the past months he hasn't
Slept much and he scarcely feels.
He is getting short, but there's little
At home. He's got few illusions.
"The world": It's hard.
There's little compassion,
And they won't understand, No
Life is hard. On point he can feel.
Fear and the threat of death
Exhilarate him. He's been
Scarred and scared and numb
For Months. But on point
He can really feel.
There's people behind him
Who depend on him.
And he's good and he cares,
Though he doesn't know
Them well. He guesses it's
Love and walks
Out on that narrow road and
He's alive
For one more night.

Robert Jost, 2006

PROLOGUE

I am upstairs when my husband Arnold calls for me. He has been home from the hospital for a year now, bedridden, paralyzed and suffering from heart failure. He is in pain all the time. I knew, we were close to the end. Since he returned from Vietnam nearly fifty years ago, he has struggled with illness; diabetes, foot and back pain, heart problems, kidney failure and severe PTSD. He is now paralyzed and is losing the use of his arms and hands. I go downstairs to his room and he simply says to me, "I'm done". His final journey will last 27 days. We tell no one. I don't try to talk him out of it. His life is miserable. He believes there is nothing to live for. It's his life to do what he wants with, and it was my desire to support him in this difficult final decision. He quits eating and takes only small sips of ice water. He will die from dehydration which put him into kidney failure and other organ failure. I bury him on February 2, 2017 at Willamette National Cemetery in Portland. He is finally at peace. Vietnam no longer has him in its clutches. He is with his warrior brothers for all eternity. He has crossed to the other side of the wall.

PART 1

Chapter 1

FINDING TRUTH

Ken Burns, the documentarian, says there is no one truth in war. But, there is a single truth for the individual soldier. Arnold, my husband, had his truth, and now that he is gone, it has become my truth, and so here I lay it out as I now see it. Arnold went boldly into war, and he went boldly to his death.

My husband, Arnold Bondley, died on January 29th, 2017 from multiple organ failure. This was caused by his exposure to Agent Orange, a defoliant used in Vietnam to kill off the jungles and to destroy rice fields and enemy hiding places. A total of four million acres (¼ of Vietnam) were sprayed. Nineteen million gallons were used during the war killing jungles, people, farms, animals and birds. It is estimated that nearly nine million people were sprayed. No one thought of the damage it could do to human beings after the war. In fact U.S. soldiers were told that Agent Orange was safe, no need to try to avoid the spraying. Some soldiers talk about how good the cool sticky spray felt on their skin as it covered them and the landscape.

Agent Orange was injected into volunteer soldiers in the early sixties. It caused skin lesions that went away in time, and scientists did not think about the toll it would take on bodies 30 to 40 years down the road. Agent Orange never leaves your body after exposure, and I believe it has killed and will kill many, many more Vietnam veterans and Vietnamese people.

In October 2017, on the PBS News Hour show, it was reported that in the Da Nang area, where Arnold was, the water and land are still contaminated with Agent Orange. The water is not safe to drink. Children living in the Da Nang area suffer from birth defects. For American soldiers who served in Vietnam, some of their children suffer from spinabifita, a neurological disease. The war continues to hurt and kill our veterans and the Vietnamese people.

Chapter 2

GROWING UP

Arnold's parents both grew up in Los Angeles. They knew each other as kids and dated occasionally as teens. Arnold's father, Russ, was drafted during WWII and was a supply sergeant in the Air Force, in Iceland. Arnold's mother, Jeanne, was a professional ballet dancer and married Russ during the war. Their lives together were troubled, and their communication with each other was never good. They lived very separate lives. Their poor communication would bleed into their everyday lives after the war.

Twenty five years later, on their anniversary, Jeanne wrote Russ a letter saying she was leaving. Their marriage was an unhappy union from the start. Although, they both dearly loved their children, Arnold, Ken, and Jennifer. I think all three kids suffered from their parents' disengagement from each other and ultimately from their children. Arnold had no adult mentors in his life. He so desperately needed one as a teenager. There was no one to give him advice or support when his draft notice arrived, at the age of 19. He had no one to talk to about being drafted and what he might have been able to do to avoid combat.

Arnold was born in Billings, Montana, and when he was four years of age, his Dad was recalled to the Air Force, during the Korean conflict, and was sent to England. Jeanne and Arnold left New York on the ship Queen Elizabeth. Arnold thought the ship was great fun. It was rough weather and he loved sliding down the isles and chasing dinner rolls as they jumped off the dining tables during those rough seas. His mother was afraid, and he gently reminded her, "Mom I will always take care of you." She remembered that, and he did always look after her, particularly after her divorce. Arnold was always a caring and devoted man to his family and friends.

When Arnold and his mother arrived in England, they rented a very large old house outside of London. They pretty much lived in the big kitchen as the house was often cold, and they burned coal in a large cook stove to keep warm. Arnold loved the snails in the yard and remembers squishing them with his tricycle. He was a little devil even at that age.

Two years later, the family would return to Billings, and Arnold's Dad went to work as a carpenter with his father. He later went to work for Chevron Oil Company as a technical draftsman. He built their first house using a load of slab rock from the hills above their house. An activity that Arnold loved and would continue enjoying into adulthood. He loved brick and rock work, and he particularly loved to build old time fireplaces. The fireplace in our second home had been designed by Benjamin Franklin. Arnold also loved outdoor brick and stone work, building fireplaces, patios and foot paths throughout our yards.

As Arnold got a little older, one of his favorite things was catching baby rattlesnakes for pets. He was showing his brave side but of course, this didn't please his parents. He also had a toy cannon that he used to wreak havoc. He shot his brother in the face with a load of blackberries. He blew a whole in the backyard fence and dug trenches in the yard. I guess he was already a warrior or thought he wanted to be.

In 1963, when Arnold was 16, his family moved to Beaverton, Oregon where his Dad continued work as a draftsman with Shell Oil Company. This was a hard move for a teenager. He left all his friends in Billings, and he became very rebellious. He was a young man who was intrigued with guns. He could shoot a nickel out of the air with an air gun, his friends told me. Arnold was an excellent sharp shooter. He took target shooting lessons from the NRA. I think that pretty much guaranteed that in 1968, he would go to Vietnam as a shooter. This skill would later help him save the lives of the Vietnamese people and U.S. soldiers. A skill that could be used for good or evil though. Arnold believed his shooting skills were mostly used for evil. "Hunting and killing. That was our job," he would say, of his squads tracking the North Vietnamese Army (NVA).

Arnold was always a kid who enjoyed adventure. He snuck out of his house starting at about age 12 and would tour his neighborhood causing all kinds of havoc including using his BB gun to shoot out house windows in a new subdivision that was being built a few blocks away. As a teenager, he and friend Tom had a still in the woods behind their houses making moonshine. Arnold and his friends also liked to find building sites where there was building equipment, tractors, dump trucks, and caterpillars. They would hot wire them and drive them around the site. He was also very smart, as he never got caught. His brother Ken was sometimes an accomplice when Arnold would sneak out of the house at night, as Ken would vouch for him should Arnold's parents become suspicious of Arnold's night time activities. His worst offense was stealing some ammunition from a local gun store. He stalked the store for weeks before breaking in. Boy, was he surprised when the story of the break in was on the front page of the Portland newspaper the next day. He quickly got rid of the ammunition in the woods behind his house, got a buzz hair cut, and bought some new stylish clothing. His parents were so proud of him for taking such an interest in his new look!

High school friends said Arnold was a prankster. They could always count on him for some fun. He was always on the lookout for mini marts and stole beer for him and his friends to take to the woods to drink. He was sometimes caught with the beer in his car by local police. But, he knew the local cops, and they would pull him over and take his beer and tell him not to drink and drive. Oh, how times have changed. He was never charged with possession or arrested. His personality was such that he could pretty much talk his way out of any kind of trouble, his friends would tell me. Those communication skills would later help him when he was in Vietnam.

Arnold purchased a 1965 Mustang in his junior year of high school. He loved that car. It was his holy grail. A forest green Mustang with black leather interior. He worked on it every weekend putting in a 289 cubic inch engine, four barrel carburettor and a solid lifter valve train. The car had a manual transmission and Arnold would race that car every chance he got. We still had the car after we married, and I loved to race that car too! We took it to the Nevada salt flats one year and had a great time racing.

In the fall of 1966, after high school graduation, Arnold enrolled in Portland Community College in the Criminal Justice program. I think he would have excelled in this profession. Unfortunately, Vietnam would take that confidence from him and send him in a very different direction. Art and architecture became his passion after Vietnam. Creativity would become his saving grace and a way to keep his PTSD at bay.

PART 2

Chapter 3

THE DRAFT

It was in early November of 1968 that Arnold, and most of his high school buddies got their draft notices. By early November, 1969 when Arnold was in training, there were heavy battles during and after the Vietnam TET offensive. Arnold's army buddy Allan reported:

"Tet lasted about three months, but in I Corp, it never really stopped. By 1970, the NVA was setting up booby traps more than fire fights."

At the time Arnold was drafted, I was a sophomore in high school. Of the approximately 150 senior boys who would graduate two years later in his class, only one student he knew would go into the Marines. Others found ways around the draft, many leaving the country to go to college, getting college student deferments, joining the National Guard or Merchant Marines, or Coast Guard, or Airforce, some leaving for Canada, or fathers using their connections to keep their sons stateside. Only one of

Arnold's friends, Gary Lamb, a helicopter pilot and Arnold saw combat. Gary was killed in 1969 in a crash landing.

Although Arnold was attending college, his parents either did not know or chose to ignore the option of student deferments for their son which would have kept him stateside for another four years. By 1972, had he been drafted, he would have been less likely to experience the extremes of combat. The war was winding down. I sometimes wonder if his parents felt military service was a duty. I'll never know because they never said, and I never asked. They could have told Arnold to promote his auto mechanic skills and building skills. He could have moved to California and joined the Air Force. He would not have qualified as a pilot because of his eye sight, but he would have likely been safer with a job on the ground.

His grandmother lived in LA, but Arnold's parents said nothing to him about moving to avoid an Army combat assignment. I have a friend who moved there for that very purpose. Arnold's parents had no advice at all and left him to his own decision. I have never understood their 'hands off' attitude. He was only 19 years old. He was a kid! My own parents would say to me, "I'm so glad we have no sons. We would never let any child of ours go to this war." My own Dad had found a way to avoid the draft for Korea, a war he was against. He and my mother had a child, ME, so he would not have to go. He would always tell me, I probably saved his life. I believe my parents were pacifists but never called themselves that. They pretty much kept their beliefs about war to themselves. People their age seemed to have little to say about war or the politics in the early sixties. It may have seemed unpatriotic to that generation. But certainly by the late sixties my father became more outspoken about the war in Vietnam. Arnold's father did apologize years later for letting Arnold enlist in the Army. For me, it was too little, too late. The damage to Arnold's mind was done, and there was no coming home from Vietnam. No peace for him after this experience.

So, Arnold went ahead, not knowing he had options and joined the army. He enlisted, so he could be discharged six months early to return to his college studies. All of his advice came from an Army recruiter. He left, feeling unsure of the purpose of the war, but when he got there, he would give it his all, doing everything he could to save the lives of his squad and later the lives of the Vietnamese people. That would be his mindset in his second and last tour – save lives. He would say as others have, "If not me, then who?" I know some of his other buddies felt that the war was wrong and their personal mission was to stay alive for twelve months, get home and forget it, which of course would not happen.

PTSD would affect some 60% of the Army and Marine infantry units. Until much later, there was no help for these veterans including Arnold. They would have to live with the horrors of Vietnam for the rest of their lives. Arnold would say he had a whole other life he could not share with anyone, including me. "It was too terrible", he said, and he would not hurt me with the details. Arnold felt his friends who did not go to Vietnam would never understand the horror of war and what he went through.

Finishing Bootcamp, 1968

Arnold did not talk about boot camp much. I know he did well, as he was both physically strong and an excellent sharpshooter. I know he did worry that some of the less fit guys would not do well in a war zone. He already worried about his fellow soldiers. But, I think he felt confident he would be okay in combat. He was good with a rifle and believed he would not be shot, and he wasn't. But no 19-year-old is thinking about the trauma of the war and what it would do to their brains, PTSD and concussions afterwards. Luckily, Arnold was an excellent shooter and managed to stay alive, but what he would see and do in Vietnam left his mind restless and would not let go of him until his death 49 years later. Arnold could be such a fun, caring and loving person, a bit radical and definitely a risk taker, but he was a good person. How I wish he could have seen that in himself.

Arnold believed he would be a good soldier when he arrived in Vietnam. He did his best during his first tour to be brave and courageous and do what the commanders wanted. When he got home he would say, "I was duped. How could I be so stupid?" During his second tour, he would not be so compliant. He re-upped for another six months so he could save more American soldiers, not to kill. Taking his squad into a deadly fire fight, he would no longer do. "Hunting humans" as he would say was no longer something he could tolerate. He never got into any trouble for disobeying orders that I know of, as he said and his friend Allan said, "The commanders were afraid of him. The commanders also would come to understand that their lives were in danger from their own troops if they made poor choices for their men going into combat. A smoke bomb in their hootch would be a warning. If they continued to make poor choices for their troops, they would be killed by their own men."

Chapter 4

PSYOPS

According to U.S. military publications, the purpose of Psyops (Psychological Operations) was to train soldiers to influence the emotions and reasoning of the enemy. "Psyops was believed to threaten, disrupt, upset and confuse the enemies' decision of making progress and to reduce the enemies' will to fight." This was Arnold's assignment. He was a psychological analyst.

Arnold said the program never worked. I believe Arnold was in a unit of black Psyops, 7th Psychological Operations Group. He participated in covert operations, spending time in North Vietnam. He was never allowed to talk or have any contact with American media.

Arnold was sent to Fort Holabird in Baltimore after Basic Training and was enrolled in Psychological Operations School. Although lonely, being so far from home, and not knowing anyone, Arnold did enjoy the classes. One of his army buddies, mentioned that they got very good at picking door locks. I wondered how many Vietnam village straw huts would have a door much less a locked door! What a useless skill to learn. Arnold was in classes for three months before leaving for Vietnam.

Chapter 5

GOING TO VIETNAM

Arnold received orders in April of 1968 that he was going to Vietnam on the ship General John Pope, a WWII troop carrier for 6000 men. He left from San Francisco in May. It would take nearly a month to get to Vietnam. The trip was miserable. Soldiers had guard duty, two hours on and four hours off, a tactic to keep soldiers tired and I suppose out of trouble. Arnold's friend Doug said Arnold guarded a soda machine, just a very ridiculous, mundane assignment. Getting adequate food was also a challenge. It would take two hours in line to get a meal of powdered eggs and toast, so Arnold used the vending machines and lived on crackers and spray cheese. They slept in hammocks stacked one on top of the other. Troop ships are very claustrophobic and that experience would stay with him the rest of his life. He could not stand to be in a tight space, and I think that is why he liked to spend so much time in the outdoors.

Arnold's good friend Doug said he and Arnold felt like robots during the three week trip to Vietnam. One night Doug and

Arnold, being a little devilish, decided on a prank. Doug wanted a coke, which they were not allowed to have while on watch. Arnold got it for him, and then he told Doug he was going to climb the 75 foot mast of the ship, and he did it, and no one saw him do it. He made it to the top, out of sight of the commanders. While this was happening, Doug was caught with his coke and was put in jail for a few hours. The next day, the ship docked at Subic Bay, Philippines for an eight hour liberty. Doug was only allowed four hours of leave.

Both Arnold and Doug would end up in Da Nang. Doug spent most of his time in Vietnam working on propaganda materials, while Arnold spent his time in combat with the Marines distributing propaganda materials to villagers and setting up loud speakers to try to scare the enemy during fire fights.

U.S Pope Troop Ship, headed for Da Nang

Chapter 6

ARRIVING AT 1 CORPS, DA NANG

There were four places in Vietnam the soldiers would get off the ship, Arnold told me, starting in the south. The further south you were, Arnold believed, the safer you would be. I don't know if that was true, as there was a lot of action in the Mei Kong Delta. I met many paralyzed Navy veterans at the Seattle VA hospital who were shot and injured on Swift boats. Senator John Kerry was on a Swift Boat and was injured three times during fire fights.

Arnold's name was not called until the ship was far north in Da Nang very near the DMZ (the border between north and south Vietnam). He writes to his family:

Here I am, Da Nang, Vietnam. We arrived Thursday afternoon around 2:00 pm. The ship tied up in Da Nang harbor at 8:00 am, Thursday morning. We had eaten breakfast, turned in our bedding and readied our gear. We were expecting to disembark at 9:00 am, as the other two groups did at Cam Rahn Bay. But, we waited and waited. We were very anxious to get off the ship. That ship became 'old' after the first three days.

At 11:00 am we ate lunch aboard the ship. We thought perhaps we'd spend the night on it, but at 2:00 pm we walked down the gang plank. They had 'cattle trucks' waiting for us on the dock. The trucks were crowded and hot. Around the box there was a 4" slot so we could see the country side. Everyone was cranked around on their bench taking the first look at their new home. It was quite shocking. The place looks like an Asian Berlin after bombing. The place was probably 'slummy' anyway. What a ruin! I'll try to paint a picture for you.

The streets are narrow and rugged with very dusty shoulders. Right off the road shoulders the houses begin. They look like they were made from junkyard scraps of tin, tar paper and old splintered pieces of wood. There's junk all over their premises. Of course, these houses are built by the families living in them. They are open on most sides for catching the cooling breezes and so no one can see into them. They have dirt floors and furnishings save for a pan or two, and clothes hanging out in the sun. The place looks worse than anything I've ever seen.

The people are small and thin, normally dressed in baggy white pants, dark shirts and those cone hats. They invariably wear thongs. Some of the kids run around naked. Quite bizarre. People urinate and excrete right off the highway so you can imagine the smells, especially in this heat. As a whole, the people look depressed. They never hurry at anything. Slow and easy going.

Arnold recalls: The climate is equally unusual. The high temperature at 3:00 pm is normally 105-110 degrees Fahrenheit. Humidity must stay at 90 percent. At 8:00 am, two hours after sunrise, the temp must be 80-85 degrees. Warm! I'll send lots of pictures.

Villagers living near Freedom Hill

Our cattle trucks went through the very crowded civilian section and then over a bridge to the military base (1st Marine Division). You could not believe the amount of concertina wire and the sandbags in use. The base is huge and the best fortified in Vietnam. The place has only been attacked once. Saigon is attacked every day!

We arrived at the reception center and dropped our gear in the barracks. These barracks are tin roofs, half plywood, half screen and wooden floors. Outside we have a trench three feet deep with sandbags and dirt filled barrels on the edges. The reason for these trenches and bunkers is because the reception station is 100 yards from the large tactical air base. They are likely to be hit by rockets at any time. There have been no alarms though.

In the barracks there are cots. We sleep in our tee shirts and field pants. Not a bit cold. During the day around 4:00 pm, our clothes are completely soaked with sweat. The cold showers feel good.

So far we have been 'in processing.' That includes, administration, finance, and the hospital. It takes about five days. Then we'll get briefings and trainings in our MOS (military occupation specialty). Ours of course was in broadcasting. We are the disseminators of all the propaganda. We'll be spread around I Corps assessing various units. Our six man team will probably be broken up. The areas are Hue, Chu, Lai, Dong Ha, Quang Tri, and Phu Bai. We don't know where we'll be going.

Arnold would end up at Freedom Hill, Hill 327 above the Da Nang airbase where he would spend the next nineteen months and in the areas surrounding it.

Doug and I will probably try to go to the same place.

Unfortunately, that would not happen.

Freedom Hill base, 1968

Vietnam isn't as action packed as we thought it would be. You can only hear artillery and bombs off in the distance. Not scary at all. That would change.

In a 2017 AARP article, soldiers talked about enduring the terrible heat of Vietnam, 120 degrees Fahrenheit in the summer months they would say, "Just breathing the air felt like it was burning your lungs." Arnold would say in a letter home:

Now, I have to tell you about sweating. Today I sweat more than I ever have before. It was so hot in the school I visited, my clothes were completely drenched in 10 minutes! I mean completely, even my belt. After half an hour I noticed my hands were wrinkled up as happens in a bathtub. Just soggy and wrinkled up! It's a lot of sweat. Here is another example: I had one of those tin movie reel boxes laying down on the stand that I had the projector on. I leaned in on my elbow and ten minutes later there was at least 18 inches of sweat in it. That is the honest truth.

When we got back here, I went to dinner and drank half a gallon of water, half a gallon of milk, a can of coca cola, and a beer. The next time I go into the field I'm going to take some salt pills in advance. I thought I was going to pass out from heat exhaustion. The boy in my broadcasting team passed out with it twice in the last two weeks.

I'll just be sitting in the office now because we have a new man coming out here tomorrow. Yes sir, my office with the fan blowing and the ice box in the next room full of sodas and cold water. What a life.

Arnold would say to me that on top of the heat, they had to carry up to 110 pounds of weapons and gear including their broadcast speakers. It is no wonder that the Viet Cong (VC) considered U.S. troops slow and easy targets. Seeing pictures of the VC, you see them in their black pyjamas with their rifle. They could so quickly fire at our troops and be gone in minutes, often jumping into camouflaged tunnels.

During monsoon season, the soldiers slept on the ground using their ponchos to help keep them dry unless the moon was out. If you used your poncho for cover it reflected light and you could be shot. There was mud everywhere. It was hard to sleep in such conditions as the VC could be very near by, Arnold would say. Some soldiers said you could hear them whispering. You seldom knew how close they were to your squad or how many VC there were. Soldiers could be on combat duty for weeks and months at a time in the jungles.

Malaria, hookworm, foot rot, leeches, ringworm, dysentery, and dealing with snakes was common. Dry socks were a luxury. I recently read that liver fluke worms infested up to 20% of infantry soldiers. They got it from eating raw fish, sometimes the only food they had access too. Fighting in the jungles often times meant going without rations, water, and ammunition for days at a time. And, the fog was so thick in the mountain terrains at times, it clung all the way to the ground. It was impossible for helicopters to know where to make supply drops. Breaks consisted of only a week or so, where you still were not safe as rockets, mortar, and sniper attacks could come at any time in the Marine compounds.

I think the only pleasure Arnold had while at Freedom Hill was being in the hootch he and his friend Allan built. It was actually a remodel of an abandoned hootch Arnold's friend Allan would tell me. They were proud of their construction techniques.

Arnold would report to his father. It was quite the home with comfy cots, a music system, a bar and the best shower in the compound, and two puppies, Arnold would brag. Shortly after the hootch was built, Arnold wandered into the supply tent and low and behold, who was there but his high school friend Tom. Tom gave him a TV which was a real score. Unfortunately, it broke two days later. Arnold also enjoyed playing cards. He and Allan taught soldiers how to play bridge. No poker for these guys! His other thrill while at the Da Nang airbase was to lay on the runway and get as close as he could to bombers taking off. He said, "I could get ten feet from the planes as they lifted into the sky. It was a thrill!"

Chapter 7

MY TIME WITH ARNOLD IN VIETNAM – BY ALLAN

Arnold's friend and confidant, Allan McMurtry wrote the following about coming to Vietnam. I suspect Arnold and Allan had many of the same experiences. As Arnold did not write much about day-to-day activities, I am thankful for Allan's willingness to share his memories of the war and his time with Arnold.

Allan: I arrived in Da Nang in late March of 1969. Arnold had been there nearly a year and was at the head quarters at the 1st Marine Division at a place called Freedom Hill. We were on a very long and high ridge south west of Da Nang. The ridge rose above us to the west maybe 1000 to 2000 feet that ran north and south. The Marines held a perimeter along that ridge, I'm fairly sure, but I don't know for a fact. For reasons unknown, we were on a beautiful perch overlooking the bay, the city of Da Nang, and Monkey Mountain across the bay with Marble Mountaintop to the south east. Beyond the mountains stretched the South

China Sea. It was a pretty amazing view. I doubt many of us enjoyed it much though.

Arnold did mention the view in his journal. As a lover of nature, one of his worst memories was the destruction that was done to the land, the whole countryside pockmarked by bomb craters. Arnold would say that he could not believe the damage he saw to the country side when he was up in a spotter plane distributing propaganda flyers. U.S aircraft destroyed jungles, farm land, and mountain villages. Pictures he showed me reminded me of the moon scape, barren and bleak. Today, I look at pictures of those areas. The land has healed itself and the bomb craters while still there are green and lush.

Arnold had established himself as the first sergeant of the outfit by the time I arrived. His task was to keep tabs on reports, monitor the teams, do what the Captain/Lieutenant needed done, and he likely gave them some sage advice. I know he was part of a team upon his arrival, but I never knew how far afield they went. We now know from Arnold's journal, he spent some time in North Vietnam.

Arnold was dead right, the two of us were on roads where the Marines went down only in force. They had check points along the roads that buttoned up at night. The Marines had outposts scattered around in clumps with Battalion Head Quarters like the 1st, 2nd, and 3rd Battalion stretching in an arch across the SE portions of Da Nang, maybe 5-20 miles out. Nobody knew where the opposition might be, and the teams on the audio trucks were shot at if they were out too late. The audio trucks which Arnold *mentioned most to me would broadcast frightening sounds and propaganda information at round ups of villagers. I think they would go north about half way to Hue. Some villages were pretty basic with hootches, some rudimentary fencing and accessible only by dirt roads. Potential for ambush abounded. It should be noted that generally speaking '66 was better than '65. '67 was better than '66 and '68. However, things were always in flux. Without a doubt things were more risky in 1968 than in 1969. The operations pace began to slack off in the fall of 1969. Operations still occurred, but there were no operational programs that were working to any beneficial end. The teams would go to the south edge of the Marine cordon and beyond, stretching onto the Khe Sanh Ridge to the south southwest. You could go south along Route 1 to the American Division south of us. I never made it there, but Arnold likely did.*

I think the actual name of the nearby village was An Hoa, the 7th Marine Head Quarters. There was also Hoi An, a beautiful seaside village/town due south of Marble Mountain maybe 20 miles. American elements were there, but I do not know who and how many. I am unaware of the bridge across the DMZ being blown up. That did not happen in my tenure.

I know from Arnold's journal that Arnold was in North Vietnam when the Liberty Bridge was blown up. He and the Marines were picked up by helicopter. Arnold said he was never so frightened that he would be captured or killed. He never discussed why the Marines and Army were in North Vietnam. Although, they were most likely chasing the North Vietnamese Army (NVA).

I think Arnold was the only team member who had much of a relationship with the officers though a team operated out of the 7th Psyops Headquarters on the first Division Head Quarters (HQ,) a big sprawling base west of Da Nang and the air base below. Based on his discussion and the frequency of operations when I first arrived, the gut wrenching aspect was the short notice to load up and head out to unknown terrain with unknown people for unknown tasks. The call to ready for a mission could come at any time.

One reason Arnold could not listen to 60s music was some of the soldiers would play music as they got ready for the next fight. Arnold always thought that this was the last music he would ever hear because thoughts of death were what they were all thinking of as they headed out into the jungle.

If you lived through the operation (all were given exotic names and would last weeks or months), which not all Psyop 7th troops did. You got to sleep on the ground, wander through the jungle, camp (ha-just gather around in a circle at night and shut your mouth), eat out of tin cans, deal with the rain, scrounge water, bullets, food, and batteries for your loud speakers and try to figure out what this cluster fuck was all about.

The Marines were close to hostile about us taking their resources. The real ass kicking about all the missions was that you had no idea what was going on, who was in charge and what their mission was. More importantly, you had no allies. To this day, I firmly believe that I had only a 50/50 chance that if we got killed, our bodies would be picked up. Arnold had been in that environment for nine months before I showed up. I had a Battle of the Bulge Vet tell me that he always felt he had to look out for himself. Yep, hard to put in words the dread each day brought, the visceral reaction to hearing the name of a new operation. I can see guys that would go bat shit crazy. I never called home and rarely wrote. If I did, I didn't talk about what I was doing. Arnold did write home but also never talked about the missions he had been on. It was all random crap that Arnold knew well, had participated in at length.

The other thing was that Arnold, by June 1969, had seen all his early buddies go home. There he was trying to make new friends from a list of new doughboys. He outlasted them all, officers included. All stuffed into one's psyche. No wonder it was still leaking out 50 years later. More history than any one person can comprehend. And, to comprehend was an outlawed word. Hell, I find myself talking out loud in the shower or at work to the point somebody will ask what the heck I said. So like a tattoo, this stuff is in there for good. I remember a few guys besides Arnold who were still there when I showed up. But, I was out into the field within 10 days and would only randomly come into HQ. The same and somewhat that Arnold did, only for a longer period of time in more adverse conditions.

I am convinced that some of the Psyop teams did things to get out of fighting a worthless battle. There were instances I suspected where guys shorted out their equipment rather than go into the field again. I know one guy was screaming out in the field with nightmare after nightmare. I know that two guys were killed shortly before I got there. I saw dead Marines laid out in the equivalent of a bar ditch (a road side channel). I'm not saying

I had it so bad, but Marines had higher casualties compared to lower causalities for the Army. If someone were to ask me "Did Arnold lie on his kill reports, I'd have to say, bottom line, that I do not believe so. He did not buy into body count as a way to measure American success. There was no measure of success.

Arnold had a lot of contact with villagers and the VC, and absolutely children were tricked into carrying grenades, and every guy in our unit knew that. Every Vietnamese person was a probably VC, men, women and children."Kill anything that moves", was the motto Arnold would explain to me. "Hunt humans. That was our job."

It was a strange thing to contemplate that the Marines were in more danger, but we were more terrified. Makes us sound like a bunch of pansy asses. The statistics will bear me out. Those killed tended to be the ones with the poorest leadership, the least amount of training, and shortest time in a platoon. That pretty much describes every one of us in every fight we went into. It makes me angry just recalling it. Why not give us infantry advanced training before shipping us oversees into combat patrols for God's sake. Arnold stayed too long in hopes he could save more Americans lives. Army basic training was eight weeks, while Marines had basic of up to 12 weeks. They learned to fire everything in their arsenal. We learned how to clean and fire the M-14. Then, they sent us to Vietnam with the M-16. In the early sixties the M-16s tended to jamb and the VC had superior Russian weapons.

Did we think so little of our soldiers that we sent them to war with unreliable equipment? How scary would it be to have a rifle that could jamb at anytime during a firefight? I wondered if that was the reason Arnold always carried a knife and a pistol.

That was the witches brew Arnold was exposed to and every other guy who went into the field. But, then that's war. The generals make the big calls on a map. The young guys go out and die. Nothing has changed other than better equipment to try to save lives. If you read about the last year of Korea, it will make you vomit. Meaningless patrols into no man's land. Over and over and over and over. Young guys dying based on a whim of somebody up the command chain.

Bottom line, if somebody asked me under oath did all of this happen to Arnold, I'd say that the situation over there was as such, and is very plausible.

The person you describe was the guy I knew in Vietnam and really by correspondence until the last two to three years of his illness. He was a really bright and observant guy, caring and multifaceted. He seemed to have a background in a number of areas from tools, to drawing, to construction, to car repair, and beyond that. A polymath in certain aspects. This is the guy I met in the Army.

I did not understand how the war had haunted Arnold. I do not understand the dementia he suffered, but I think the war played a role there, though I have a hard time believing it. Whether it was Agent Orange or God knows what, at his age I don't believe he was a candidate for dementia. I think guilt and PTSD took a massively heavy toll as he tried to move through personal analysis. Just how wounded are the soldiers coming back from wars is a closed book. PTSD is the first attempt to quantify it. But we have not scratched the surface. I don't consider it random that out of the twelve young guys I was with, all but three from the Army have passed away.

The curse of Vietnam is that so many men did not have to serve. So many that they don't want to talk about it. We know the stories they say, but they don't get what it was like to be carted off to boot camp following a successful physical and then drug around the country to various camps learning your MOS (Military Occupation Specialty) then being shipped one person at a time to Vietnam. It couldn't get more lonely or disorienting. The process of adapting was never complete in my opinion. People lived for the 366th day, or they didn't.

The person you describe was the guy I knew in Vietnam. And the guy I knew until the last two to three years. Really bright, really observant and caring. Really talented. He had a background in so many areas. Though I did not volunteer, I was lucky to be stationed with men who came out of the intelligence services like Arnold. "The Best and Brightest" book presented an accurate description of who I met in the services. Indeed the best and brightest.

I am so sorry you lost Arnold and the way and reasons it happened. Several of us pleaded with him to get out of Vietnam. Arnold had been there too long. I can now only imagine how soldiers on both sides have struggled with long terms of service over there. Soldiers would say, "If you stay you will be dead or crazy". The Marines did 13 months and the Army did 12. Arnold did 19. Only recently, reading your emails and Arnold's writing have

I come to understand the issues behind his emails. In my opinion, being married to a soldier with PTSD is almost as bad as having it, and the repercussions will only slowly recede.

I know you miss Arnold, and I'm glad you do. It may seem strange, but it speaks of the core of who he was and why you would miss that.

I don't know how practical one can be when faced with such a loss as you have suffered. Arnold talked about the girl he would marry. Pretty, bright and honest. I remember honest. It just so happens that I remember this discussion in our hootch late one night. He was not going to settle for less. He got what he wanted in spades.

I can't ease your pain. I can't even share the load because it isn't a zero sum game. There is more agony than all of us can handle. I remember the verse about the lilies in the field, the rejuvenation, the hope, the beauty. My Dad stayed around until age 99. I think in large part because he was optimistic. I'm sending you optimism with this letter. Optimism in your talents. A sense of well being that you have helped so many in your life. That you got to live in such a wonderful place as Oregon and sitting at your dinning table watching the ocean; friends who are there at the end of a telephone wire. You are the north star. And, your friends have commitments to your life almost as deep as it is to theirs. Among the pomp and ceremony, the sadness, tears, the individual solitude of Arnold's funeral was a nucleus of people who chose to stand in the mist and rain of a winter day in Oregon to recognize Karen and her Arnold. They stood in the ceremony to be there for you. You remain wrapped in their arms.

Undoubtedly, there are things I don't know about Vietnam, but then I think I know too much. Arnold continued some of the recklessness he had before Vietnam well into his later years based on what I know one can only absorb so many affronts to their ethical system before it changes them or their defense mechanisms. Arnold's intelligence allowed him to cover up a lot to me. He did not succeed with you. But, I consider Arnold to be a casualty of the Vietnam war.

I always thought Arnold was embarrassed by his PTSD. Maybe though it was cowardly to talk about his emotions about the war. In 2018, I received a letter from the VA that Arnold did die of a combat related illness. Agent Orange would take him from me, and it continues to take the lives of more and more Vietnam veterans.

Allan goes on to say: I was so lonely and disoriented in Vietnam. The process of adapting was never complete in my mind. Guys lived for that 366th day. One has to understand how bad some of the battles in WWII were. But, at least they had friends dating back to basic training, and they went overseas as units. We did not. We went alone to our Vietnam station. The idea of one man surviving from Normandy to VE day is pretty fantastical. Those soldiers had a one month shorter tour than a regular tour in Vietnam and only 60% of Arnold's tour.

Reading about Laos will make you want to tear your hair out. Then reading about the Cambodian killing fields, you realize that U.S. troops never did things done in Cambodia. Our record with the CIA is less praise worthy as junior cowboys and Rambos ending up causing the Vietnamese Hmong decades of grief.

I recently asked Allan if he was going to watch the Ken Burns special about the Vietnam War.

Allan replied: No, I'm not watching it. A friend was talking to me about it, and I realized I was getting agitated. I was opposed to the war before I was drafted. Nothing changed other than more evidence I was correct.

In April of 2018, Allen wrote to me about his continued thoughts about Vietnam and his recent trip to the Amarillo Army Base.

Allan wrote: As for me, I am still working on impressions about returning to the Examination and Induction Center in Amarillo 50 years later. All in all, I'm very glad I went. Something just kept pushing me as the time got closer. It did bring back a lot of memories. And, they weren't all bad. Some melancholy, sure. But overall, I was able to recreate some of the old feelings. It actually felt good at times and, at other times, it made me angry, then sad. With the passing of the guys I knew best, I guess I was paying respect to them, maybe lamentations that we were caught up in that stupid war.

I did make it to the current Military Entrance Processing Station in Amarillo. I met a 1st Sergeant (6 stripes) and a Lt. Commander in the Navy. They were very proud of their station and were stunned to get my email and actually see me arrive in person. The original site of the Entrance Examination Center is a big Salvation Army facility. How ironic. Maybe they are saving more people than the Army. I also made it to the grounds of my Basic Training area at Logan Heights at Ft. Bliss that evening after taking a flight to El Paso. The area is now an E7 housing area. Nice homes, great views. Ft. Bliss is a huge base. Just me on one of the largest military bases in the world if you include the missile range to the north. No other civilians were walking the areas I walked in. I got in easily because of the young man behind the counter became an instant friend when he found out I was a Vietnam vet coming back exactly 50 years later. His uncle had been in I Corps as well. As I left I told him to give my regards to his uncle. At 71, I don't feel that old. God knows what I looked like to him. I also got a chance to see the language school area on Biggs Field. Three barracks, a few concrete block buildings were all that was left.

I saw much of the same at Ft. Lewis Washington where Arnold was in boot camp. Not much left now that McCord Airforce base has been combined with the Army base, a few old buildings, but mostly newer construction.

As I walked the old Defense Language Institute Support Command, with the buildings still there, I walked the hall where Chuck, Herb, and I stayed at. It was not the same. The location was there, but the friends were gone. They had left a few months past 49 years ago. Chuck had passed away. I could not bring him back. I could see him at the the buildings that were gone, but new soldiers walked the area. They were bigger, more intense. I went to a 7-11 store on base right where some of the buildings used to be. It wasn't there in 1968. My army was more tied into WWII and Korea. With the draft they didn't have to impress anybody.

We were their chattel to the degree they wanted to direct or command us. I could tell that rank was still evident, but the wooden gym and library were gone. So were the clothes of that era, the green khaki pants, and green blouses. The stupid limped baseball hats and black polished boots. Ramsaur, Will, Guerrero, all gone. I could bring them back only when I closed my eyes. I couldn't get my eyes to understand that we were in the right place at the wrong time. There were no voices or echoes of voices. No concrete block house close to the runway, no tower. No chain link fence you could walk around to climb into a Cessna 150. No Mckee. No ready rooms for the contingent of would be pilots.

By 1972, it was a Master Sergeant School. I do not know how many classes followed mine. The Marines would pull back to Da Nang by February of 1970 to the degree that the U.S. Army took over continuing live fire south of Hue. In some ways Arnold saw the tsunami flow backwards, I saw the ruble it left. I do not regret getting to Vietnam in 1969 because I knew time was my friend. They had to get me back by March of 1970. For Arnold, they had no such obligation. He could opt to stay longer. So I stayed on the runway, awaiting take off while studying Vietnamese. We all did in that class, 8-5, no KP, no marching to amount to anything. For nine months there was this small island on the eastern edge of Ft. Bliss that is essentially washed away by the volunteer army. Better barracks, better training, unit commands, goals, and direction. We were like the broomsticks in Fantasia, marching up the stairs and back. Indeed, to the incantation of the Sorcerer.

What is left in Vietnam is precious little. The humidity, likely the smell of open garbage, but maybe not. The French Hotel just off the wharf a few blocks. But, it may have been long removed

41

for taller buildings. The 1st Marine Division and the wooden hootchs are likely somebody's house somewhere. The generators and portable showers gone, the cans of human waste are gone. They would be set afire probably dumped in the ocean. Maybe a few flat spots exist, and maybe you could get some conveyance out to Hill 55 and to An Hoa. I would not expect to see much else, besides the air base. Is it a commercial airport now? I don't know. The flying twin engine push-pull cessnas have left as have the F-4s and the C-35s. We were so impermanent over there. We brought it back piece meal to the U.S. Arnold has some of it, Steve and me. Some of it stuck to us in good and bad places. Arnold and Steve had it worse than I did, and I had it worse than 85% of the other combat guys. An ill wind blew over us there. It didn't bring all of us back.

I missed the understanding of its impact on Arnold, but you didn't, and I think I don't fully understand its impact on Steve. He does, Sheri does. And, another minute passes. If you want to get an idea of what it was like for Arnold, I'm your your best conduit, and a poor one in many aspects. It maybe in his pictures and mine. It is in his letters and his life. They mark both place and time. Vietnam has moved on. Nobody under age 55-60 remembers much of it. And, the world of the individual Vietnamese was very small, as small as where they could walk or if lucky take a small motorbike. It was a small world for the combat soldier.

Vietnam isn't where you will find your answer.

I spent time in Da Nang in the spring of 2019. I felt an intense need to go there, to see, smell, and feel Vietnam. I don't know what I expected, but I knew it wouldn't be closure. I am not sure what was driving this need, but going there did bring me some peace.

It was very different for me seeing the country rebuilt, with the people who are so forgiving and kind. They have moved forward, maybe because of their Buddhist beliefs, that fate guides our lives. There is no reason to think about the past; but live for today and the future. The war was fate, meant to be. There is no one to blame.

Allan wrote: I'm looking for a couple of books, U.S. Marines in Vietnam by year. It should be doable. I think sitting down with Arnold's slides and mine would be hard, but if I don't do it, I'll lose it all. I'd be guessing on some of his photos, but not much of mine. I have the maps that were declassified maybe 5-10 years ago. I've kept my slides in a dark place for almost 50 years. They have not aged. If you want to be in Vietnam in 1968 and 1969, that is the trip you take, you to Austin or Nancy and I to Lincoln City. I say that with a lot of hesitation, but worry that for all the agony, the road less traveled disappears. Your call. Do you want to walk down that road one photo at a time? I offer, and I cringe. But if you need to exorcise the ghost of the past and understand where Arnold was to the degree I can interpret it. That door is slowly swinging closed. I can't say you won't go, but if you do it, it will be for a different closure I think. None of us wanted to be there. There was nothing to find of ourselves that we already didn't know when we got there, and it might be the same for you.

The wind was blowing that day in Amarillo, and it made it much lonelier, pretty much the same feeling I had 50 years before. We all knew we would split up upon graduation at Basic and at

Language School. All and all, it was a lonely war, you know. You had friends but missions and orders and campaigns sent us up in different directions on a regular basis. Hard to believe the experience. But, we can't wonder for long, because there are really no answers. Hold your head up, put one foot in front of the other. I hope Steve and Arnold felt the pride of having answered a call. Such a waste of the right of the government to ask that a citizen come to the aid of his country. But, I doubt if any WWI, WWII, or Korean vets felt much differently. Maybe the volunteer Army is different, but I doubt it. Battle fields are all the same, I think. They are more of a time than a place, and I could sense that on my trip. I turned around before I drove off Biggs Fields, looked at the old barracks and said, "Goodbye old friend." I'm not sure who I was talking to, an artefact of who I was with people I liked I guess.

Dealing with the War

Allan wrote: If I knew how humans are supposed to deal with war, I'd be first in line to explain it all. As I told a friend, anything I say about the war is a one time series of sentences to the listener, then it is over. For me that sentence describes emotions, images, and recollections that are as vivid today as they were on the first moment, and they remain that way, popping in and out of my mind at random and awkward times. The second time I restate some war story, it is old hat to the listeners, but it is as vivid as nightmares to me. It's not like I'm unique, and everybody assimilates events differently. Thing is, I cannot describe the feelings accurately enough to convey the deeper levels of psychic *turmoil. Today is Sunday, roughly 50 years ago I was in the last amphibious assault of the Vietnam War. A couple of civic issues came up and I thought, maybe now is the time I tell people I was in Vietnam. They need to cinch their belts and take a stand, be tough. A little voice in my head kept saying no, no, no. I think the little voice is right. One very good friend argued that maybe you can't quite convey all the feelings, but it is important for others to know the best stories as you can describe. Rereading some of my comments to you several months later just illustrated how impossible that task is. I laid out segments for you, something I have not done with anybody else. There was a good reason for it. First you are Karen, and second you are trying to help other wives of vets cope. Yet I found a number of my explanations wanting. Just like I will with this letter when, and if I reread it days or months hence. I didn't get that quite right.*

So, and this sounds sophomoric, and it may well be, as I try to seal this in a capsule. Here was the time when I was picked up by a bus and ultimately sent to a war zone literally half way around the world over the course of two years. It happened to about 2.2 million, mostly guys. The U.S. was a seething pot of fear among young men and their families. Some did things I'm sure they regret to avoid Vietnam. I on the other hand I met hundreds who did not. I was talking with a lawyer the other day. "You know," he said, "there were about five people in law school who didn't come from advantaged backgrounds." He found it disgusting. I felt the same way when I dropped out of the same law school he went to. But when I got drafted, I met the rest of the USA. For me, to this day, they represented the best and the brightest. I won't say the Vietnam War was the right way to go, but on Friday I sat down with five Vietnamese for a seven course meal. Among them was a priest, two business associates, and a good friend. They all came here around 1975 fleeing communism. I haven't sat down with a single member of my law school class since the day I dropped out. Is that ironic or is that a simple step to be with those of a common bond of shared values. I'd like to think it is the latter. Freddy, Chuck and Arnold. Three guys I vowed to stay in touch with. And, of those three, Arnold was the closet by far.

So, the capsule doesn't hold, sure. Arnold found that out, Steve knows it. The price of keeping it at bay varies from time to time and day-to-day. It isn't heroic, it's just a god damned fact. You carry it around, it chews on you, you chew on it. When I get tired or feel defeated, I drag it out and look at it. It used to fire me up. I remind myself that I was there, I showed up, I was with some seriously honest and brave men. Yes, I was among cowards and cheats, but they pale in comparison. In some respects it is clearer now, I understand the history better. I understand how things operated, what the Army was set up to do, that nothing was personal, god forbid. It was just random violence in unfamiliar surroundings with strangers. At 19, few were prepared to deal with that.

Is there a point to this writing? There should be, maybe you see it, maybe it is there. Who knows. What I can say is that I admire and respect you. I know what you feel through what I feel and my shared experiences with Arnold. Then again I don't know any more than you can fully understand how I feel. But, we are two parts of a single puzzle, and you are never far away in my thoughts. When I think of Vietnam, Arnold pops, then you, then Steve, Chuck, Freddy, Gonzalez, McMillan, Wright and the long *list goes on. Some have died. Some died there. Some only died a little there. Some came back, some tried and failed, some spent it all there and came back in name and number only. In the final analysis, I just flat could not bring myself to look at pictures of the new Da Nang. I'm glad you went. I'm stunned you did. I'm happy that it helped you so much. That's what you were hoping for. For me, I was there yesterday and the day before, and last week, and the two months prior and so on.*

When I think of friends who didn't go because they drew a high lottery number, went to ROTC, went to college or grad school, were physically unfit, got a bogus doctor's diagnosis. I just stuff that into the capsule. I suspect that as time goes on, the war will claim more victims. I read where somebody close to Nixon persuaded him that an all-volunteer Army would lessen the political blowback. They didn't want anybody looking over their shoulders any more when they sent young men and now women to war. No families or vets or whoever. That way all the fear is dropped on 1% of the population—insignificant. Problem solved. So, we are petering out, those who know the clasp in the throat from the sight of the letter from the draft board, who sighted in rifles on windy days or cold days or weary days. Soon, only those who volunteered will be around, and the 1% will care.

Chapter 8

THE LETTERS (2009)

Arnold's letter to Allan

During our phone conversation, I reflected on how little perspective I had during those years of my life. You mentioned the lack of knowledge of the big mission or the grand plan, and I suddenly realized our little world was isolated from the planning and strategic planning and the strategic arm of the forces. Damn, we didn't know much.

The sage advice I remember getting from the old boys in boot camp was keep your mouth shut, don't ask questions and never volunteer for anything. Yeah, yeah, yeah. I didn't ask much in the way of questions, but I did run my mouth way too much. "Okay wise guy, go pick up cigarette butts for 19 hours."

I had no curiosity about the big picture in Vietnam. Now, I'd be stopping in my tracks and asking just what the hell is going on here. And, I have more skill dealing with people. That is good. I've learned something. Now I wonder what I am missing in my present state of awareness. So, I learned not to ask questions and just did what I was told to do. Your want a report? You got a report. There was flexibility in how that played out, but nobody needed to know anything, and I said nothing, like a little kid testing the line.

And if some son-of-a-bitch wanted to use our broadcast team to draw fire during an operation, we had protocol. You knew the beauty of the short circuit and only a few did. "Amplifier dead. No sound, see? Bring 'er on in, and we'll send it to Saigon." We might not have a standby unit. Saigon was out back in the storage shed and who knew how long it would take to get it back. "How long will it take? We'll need a week. Okay, we'll have it fixed in a week." New fuse. But if needed, for a legitimate reason, we could have it out there on time. But that was something I learned long before the Army days. You can't beat a man at his own game.

I was surprised when you mentioned Reytter getting his leg blown off. You first mentioned that a few years ago, and I thought you must have had the name wrong. Reytter played bridge with us. That guy? He was livid when we beat them, and I thought he was going to pull his .45 on us. Not really.

I am catching a memory of the guy you were talking about. I remember doing something about him. Damn, if I can remember exactly what but, we fixed his wagon. Most likely got him transferred out of our unit.

Our talk brought out the reflection on the war experience. It's good, but it's somber. I want to discuss it more and work out the details.

The jeep was a symbol of the independence we had in the context of the oppressive regime of military service. I got it soon after I arrived, and it was all mine. I had access to all vehicle numbers in the entire region (I don't remember how). Army and Marine, and it wasn't on the list. The numbers had been changed, so I assume it had been destroyed. How did I keep it? I don't know now. It was nicer than any at the 1st Marine Division, and I parked it out front; that is to say I never hid it. Guess I just didn't parade it around.

The Jeep

Arnold further wrote to his father about stealing vehicles that could help him in his job.

I'm really catching on to this job. I've managed several 'brownie points' in the last week. As you know, in the Army acquiring equipment is a major job. That's part of mine. You have to 'steal' it normally. I guess it's not really stealing because it's all being used in the war effort. The person with the fastest hands gets the job done the best! One of the team leaders needed a fan for this truck. The ¾ ton was sitting at battalion for the last three weeks waiting for one to come from the states. My friend Larry couldn't go for this, so one night he went down to the motor pool and lifted one from a brand new ¾. The next day he was back on the job. We know that new truck would have been sitting at the motor pool for the next three months anyway. Good work Larry!"

Today I had a to run several errands trying to gather needed supplies. I noticed my jeep was about to fall apart. The differential was just about scraping the pavement. Normally fixing something like that takes about two weeks, so I wheeled in and told the CO (Commanding Officer) I wanted a new jeep, right now! That got them in gear! As you know the jeep has two differentials. Well it seems they are interchangeable. So they just put the front one in the back and the back on in the front. So much for that. I've got a new jeep!

Allan's Response:

Looks like this got a little long on me. Kinda rolled out. Lots more where this came from.

Even then, I too was bothered that I didn't have a feel for objectives. We'd sent teams out, and I bet not one of them knew what the hell they were supposed to do. One day, we were on an operation. The Marine Major was pissed because the Vietnamese villagers would not come line up. He asked Pham Van Minh, our interpreter, if he could do something. We were live, so Minh says a few things and people come out of their hootch's, carrying things. Now, my Vietnamese was occasionally useful. I knew enough to know I could make the other Vietnamese laugh when I talked. But, a few words and the major's reaction didn't seem right. So I asked Minh what he said. He told them that if they weren't out in ten minutes, planes would come and napalm them. The Major was happy. I was furious. I had a discussion with 17-year-old Minh about how we weren't making friends by threatening to bomb them. He thought he had done a good job. He quickly became confused. The difference was the Major wanted results right then. We wanted results over time.

Marines 1. Psyops 0. Marines killed in action 14,000+ in our area. It wasn't like we didn't try.

I read a little about Vietnam and was highly dubious about the whole war. Nothing was making sense. If I had read the New York Times (Halberstram) in 1962, I might have left for Canada, though that was not the family's style, and I might embarrass my folks and grandmother. As it was, I had been offered a position in the U.S. Army band and had turned it down which lead to my later escapades in Da Nang. I wasn't the bravest guy, out there by a mile, but like you, I'd do my duty, without, thank you very much, volunteering for jack shit which was also advice I had been given.

How I ended up in language school is still a mystery to me to this day, this very minute. Everyone in that school was regular army, but me. At 23, I had a jaundiced view of the military and the rampage in Vietnam that clashed with guys at the Language Institute at Fort Bliss. I made about as many enemies as friends,

I guess. But I got lucky and got put in with the senior NCO for nine months. Five of us were privates add the other four were E6-9 (ranks). We used the Officer's name to get little favors. We did it and figured we could explain his standing orders to do what was good for the Army. Three of us in the same room were "good for the Army", so we arranged this and that. And, if inspections by the supercilious Lieutenant, we'd mention to the Top that we had studies to do. He wasn't a fool, but he loved his command voice and showing us he could have sent us to Hell if he wanted. Crazy me, I kept a 22 automatic in the trunk of my car, highly unusual for an enlisted man. But, the inspections lieutenant never thought of combing through my car.

I noticed you were well aware of efficacy of reports. That was one thing that tipped me off to your skills. That made a lot of sense. They want reports, then by God, they would get reports. To me, that meant that nobody would bother us. It appeared you had learned that by osmosis. I actually got quite a kick out of your pea under the walnut shell trick (they thought you were in one place, but you were somewhere else, safer). It worked so well, you kept HQ totally off our backs. And, I know you knew that. Now I see that is a lot for a 20-year-old to know at that time. You had the right amount of brains and the recipes. I have to believe the officers loved the hell out of you. Team needed to be sent somewhere – DONE. Reports needed to be made – DONE. Officers needed asses covering – DONE. Officers wanted good advice – DONE. I think you were more cynical at that time than I was. In the back of my mind, I kept thinking we could do something of import. Toward the end of my tour, I had given up on that. Here we were moving around the countryside, taking rocket fire at HQ, awaiting whatever might come out of the night sky and for what? I figure the sum of what we did was a piss in the whirlwind. It still bothers me to this day. Maybe the best we did was to not send any body bags back to the U.S. We had our teams out there. We did as asked. If called, a team showed up anywhere they wanted us, any time.

Arnold did not always follow orders and at times took his team away from fire fights. That was his shell game con.

I was with the Marines, 2nd battalion, 1 Regiment. The Lieu-tenant yells at me to set up the M-60. Well, I've never set up an M-60. He started cursing. I started to tell him to tell the VC shooting to give up. But I found out that officers generally were were below clear headed thinking. Blow hards with the Military Code of Justice right behind them. In fairness, they did have responsibilities, and I knew that. Some handled them well. Some really struggled. Take the cursing. Get them later if you have a chance and felt they deserved it. Still like you said, it was somber times. And, this and a lot of the memories are somber. Maybe some personal doubt, maybe a little melancholy or depression. At the same time, the Psyop units had few friends outside our scat-tered units. I often wondered if we were shot dead if our bodies would be picked up, seriously. The tenor of the author of "Death Valley" took was one of derision at the Psyops Captain trying to make things happen. He mentioned in passing that the Captain had the lower portion of his leg blown off later. I know that was wrong. He had bogus information.

I'll never forget that bridge game. You were absolutely chomping at the bit to tear into those guys. I felt like I was being hustled by a carny as you whispered in my ear outside the building about how you would set them up. I can't remember if you told them we'd kick their asses. I do remember the dawning on their faces as they took a pasting from us. Can't say for sure, but I think we beat them, 2-0 and 2-1. Anyhow, I spent most of my time watching you. I was leery of what the Lieutenants were going to do. As I recall, we were in the building next to our hootch. I thought maybe one of the officers was a Marine. After the shellacking and awkward discussion, I couldn't help wonder what they were thinking. After all, this was a God damn Army Intelligence Operation. Did they think we were morons or something? Well you play with fire...I thought you were going to get us shot all right. You bent the line between officer and enlisted/draftee pretty severely. I was glad to leave HQ later on, wondering if you'd be killed in your sleep. I think you said it humbled them a little, but I cannot recall exactly.

As for fixing the jerk, you might be right. As I think about it, you were not fond of him. But I can't remember what you might have done. Knowing you, it would have been talking up an opening back at HQ in Da Nang. But you are right he did leave for other places.

You didn't come through HQ in Da Nang because you were there before that guy probably existed. When I came through there, I thought most the guys were jerks. I assumed that was just the way it was going to be. Nobody seemed to care whether the new guy got food or water or not. When the Captain or Major at HQ took the two of us new guys into his office to determine our future, the guy who tore up my hand launched into a long exploitive why we would be an asset right there at HQ. The implication was I could take my mangled hand to report, and we'd all be in for it. I'm sure I told you how you can get a sense of things and figure you are better off going with the current rather trying to make decisions based on little information. I'm not sure what my motives were. I think the only motive I had was to at least show and do what I was asked to without complaint. Don't get me wrong. I would have gladly stayed at Psyop HQ in Saigon if they had shown me a typewriter, but I had pretty much been assured I was not going to be typing. I can't say I knew that for sure upon arriving in Vietnam.

Thing was, when somebody from Psyops at the 1st Marine Division HQ picked me up, and it was likely you, I noticed a much more laid back attitude, dirty boots (which I wanted right then and there to show I was tough as nails, but found out later that would take two to three months to get that dirty) much friendlier, more inclusive and more open. I think the guys picking me up wanted nothing more than to piss into the mess kits of the guys at Da Nang HQ before leaving as soon as their bladders were empty. That is the way I felt. So, I was actually a little less apprehensive once I got into the ¾ ton truck for ride back out west.

On arrival, I found that the guys there didn't have their personal maids, special areas of make believe, pecking order based on deodorant choice. They had some booze, some cards, some actual combat experiences, and a sense of camaraderie. Nobody kissed me, but they didn't treat me badly. I liked that atmosphere better even though I was something like 10-14 days away from my last wake up call. I would say I was dizzy to the max. So any friendly unassuming faces were most welcome. The card games *at night, bridge of all things, really was my salvation, a way to get involved and get to meet some guys willing to pass judgement after they had some information.*

After an hour or two of cards one night, you particularly seemed to decide to find a little bit more about me. That sure made a difference, you just can't know. I can still see that hootch this day, and where we played cards, and the sense of slight belonging that came with playing that night. All of a sudden I had a chance to prove myself, small step by small step. And, that was my first toe hold into Vietnam. Arnold's head cock at a bid or card play I don't remember which. I was home. Funny isn't it, what little niche we carve out to claim a spot and how hard we can cling to it for sanity.

I'd like to flesh out some of the details. It has been 40 years. On the button. You believe that. I had some proud moments back then when I surprised myself and some not so proud moments when I failed or made a wrong decision when none of them were good. I never really wrote back home much after the first couple of months. I never called. I don't know why. And, I never realized how badly my family suffered while I was gone. Only recently has my brother mentioned some things. A few sentences out of the blue regarding my Mother, something regarding my Dad, and even some of his feelings. I am very slowly getting a very distant picture of the fear and sadness that fell upon my folks when I left. I kind of cloak that, as near as I can from unasked questions, wrapped them up in their own imagination. Damn, nobody comes back the same to the same people do they?

I figure we played out that war in aspects of our lives since then, and will likely do it for the rest of our lives. I have often thought the real challenge of analyzing that part of my brain's memory is to accept what took place without judgement, either over wrought or under appreciated. Try to understand the incomprehensible and see if some of how that will set my backbone to achieve again, what I thought I did well and to improve upon the failures without shivering. No easy path to trod in some respects, but then again we were goddamn young and still undertook an uncertain present and foreboding future. I think the worse of a two dimensional perspective, we should recognize that in as much as decisions are made by those who showed up, we showed up. A little quiet self respect for that alone is probably, given the circumstances over there, long overdue.

Your friend in all circumstances.
Allan

Chapter 9

THE JOURNAL

A rnold started PTSD therapy in 2010. He kept a journal during his three years of therapy. I found it a couple of months after his death, staring at me from a bookcase, saying take me and make me real. What I write is what he wrote along with comments from myself and friends as I felt he was much too hard on himself. "War is hell" as they say, and Arnold had no luck in forgiving himself for participating in the Vietnam war and for the killing he did.

First impressions of Vietnam

The area outside Da Nang was active, with the units of the First Marine Division on alert, and, I was on the wire perimeter of Hill 327, Freedom Hill. The valleys and hills below, were both close in and distant. The night skies were illuminated by dozens of flares, some very large bombs dropped from C47s along with artillery.

Our perimeter was not lit, so we were under the cover of shadows, and we had a panoramic view from our elevated position.

My team duties were to make friends with villagers who were borderline friendly to U.S. troops. These villages received rice rations. In the evenings, the team would a set up projectors so villagers could watch cartoons, a John Wayne movie along with a propaganda film. Sometimes the villagers clapped when we arrived and shot at us as we left.

Arnold wrote about one of his experiences:

It is 6:00 pm and I'm finally back from the operation I went on this afternoon at 12:00 pm. It was quite an experience. We, the broadcasting team, were obligated to show cartoons at a village located about ten miles south and west of our division, between Charlie Ridge and Mortar Valley. We were to get protection from the 3rd Battalion of the 7th Marine Regiment when we got there. We arrived at about 1:30 pm and picked them up. There were about six of them plus our team of two. Off we tore, screaming down the narrow dusty, and very bumpy Vietnam country roads at about 40-50 miles per hour. These roads have mines implanted in them what is known as command mines. Charlie just presses a button when a prime vehicle comes along and bang! Needless to say, I was just a little unsure of myself. I was driving and Lt. Bano was riding shotgun, looking for snipers. The Marines sweep these roads every morning, but Charlie is able to plant goodies in them during siesta time or during slack times in the traffic. So nobody knows what can happen.

Heading off to a movie show

When our B team began broadcasting to the population that a movie was going to be shown in the school house in about ½ an hour. Fifteen minutes later there were about 200, no exaggeration, kids piled around the jeep. I managed to set up the projector despite the kids dangling from my fatigue jacket. Finally the cartoons started at the announced time, and the kids went wild, even though a ⅓ of them were unable to see. I just sat back dripping with sweat and watched the cute little kids.

My tour guide, Trinh, in Vietnam says her grandparents remembered the movies. And, I thought that was my Arnold!

These kids had never seen a cartoon before or even a movie for that matter, so they were very intrigued with the whole thing. As I said there were about 200 kids, ages two to 13 or 14. When the first reel of three were through and intermission was in process I had about 50 helpers trying to expedite the process of rewinding the film. These kids would soften the hardest heart with no exception. I struggled on and when I finally switched the power on again, the crowd just exploded with happiness. You should have seen it. I tell you it was quite an experience.

After the movies, I decided to distribute some Chieu Hoi balls. These are two inch plastic balls that are painted yellow with the words Chieu Hoi (meaning open arms given to NVA soldiers wishing to surrender). They are items of propaganda but the kids, as I found out today, go crazy over them. It just so happened I took along about 400 of them. It was a good thing I didn't take only 50 of them, which was the case most of the time. The kids were beginning to scatter when I threw a couple to some lonesome little girls who were standing and watching me. All of a sudden these scattered kids once again turned into a mob and I was covered. I threw Chieu Hoi balls until my arm ached. And, then I just kind of lobbed them. I don't know where the balls went, unless there were 200 more kids because it seemed like there were 200 kids left who were Chieu Hoi ball less. A kid with one of those balls was the happiest kid I have ever seen in my life. One of those stupid little balls held more than Christmas ever held for any kid in the U.S., I swear. Really an experience.

As no one really knew who exactly was friendly and who were the enemy, it was most likely, they were both. These villagers were just trying to survive. The Americans appeared to them to be evil giants (the average Vietnamese man is about five feet tall). Americans had sophisticated armored vehicles, large bomber planes and artillery helicopters that could get low and shoot easily into the forest and villages. They were especially afraid of the flame throwers used to burn people in their straw huts and tunnels.

Villagers lining up for rice rations

Because the villagers received some food rations, they might begin to trust the U.S. soldiers. Yet in the following days or weeks, that village could be napalmed by Air force bombers.

In my mind, there was no sense in these Psyop missions. Arnold's' team also set up loud speakers during battles to broadcast frightening sounds (wandering soul sounds. Dead fathers calling for their children). This was very dangerous work, as the VC would shoot at the speakers and the Psyop teams around the area. Meanwhile, the Marines could go to a different part of the fight area giving them an advantage. In time, Arnold would learn to analyze the mission they were being sent on, and if it seemed to him a death mission for his squad, he would take his men away from the fighting. The Marines seemed not to care about him doing this. There was no love lost between the Army and the Marines. There seemed to be little collaboration between the two.

Thought I would mention something about the loud speaker teams. These guys are the toughest guys in the service here. They are really rugged. They have to be because they have a price on their head. The NVA offer $500 for each man that is captured. One of the things the NVA wanted ceased in the war is "the use of psychological operation commandos". These guys are a walking arsenal. They all have bayonets, K-bars (knives), M-2 Carbines, M-14s and plenty of ammunition. Some have BARS (Browning automatics), grease guns (automatic 45s and Thompsons). Where they get them from I'll never know. Two of the guys have sawed off shotguns. Rough bunch.

Chieu Hoi (Open Arms)

The Chieu Hoi program was a way for the U.S. and South Vietnamese Army to encourage defection of the North Vietnamese soldiers. In 1967, the military reported that 20,000 NVA and VC had surrendered where they were taken to Saigon for safety and education purposes. Some people doubt these numbers.

Chieu Hoi Surrender Program

The Chieu Hoi program had problems, the Americans making propaganda flyers often did not understand the culture of the Vietnamese and unintentionally made offensive statements.

For Arnold, this was a very difficult program for him to promote, as most likely any NVA and VC surrendering would be shot. Some U.S. soldiers called Chieu Hoi, "target practice". Another thing that would happen would be the captured VC would be loaded into a helicopter and taken up and thrown out of the chopper. As Arnold saw more and more of this, he took his Chieu Hoi cards and flyers out in a plane and dumped them into the ocean. The balls he gave to children to play with. Arnold was learning to save lives.

Chapter 10

DISABILITY

Arnold saw so many atrocities. He would report some of them on this disability claim. It took him two years to gain the courage to report what he saw and did. And, as he said, everyday there had its trauma. He never knew if he would live or die when he was sent out of the Marine compound. And, even the compound was dangerous, as the NVA would invade the camp occasionally and fire fights would ensue.

Applying for Disability

In 2009, Arnold would apply for disability for PTSD, diabetes, and hearing loss. It would take him two years to complete the application. He could not bear to write what he had experienced, what he had done. It became more than just thoughts. It became real again. Applying for disability is a hard thing for soldiers to do. It made Arnold feel vulnerable and not valued for what he did accomplish.

Arnold Guarding the perimeter of Freedom Hill

Arnold recalls: "Day two in the Marine compound at Freedom Hill, I was on guard duty at night and I kept seeing a head popping up on the the other side of the concertina wire. I waited and waited hoping he would leave. When that did not happen, I shot the head off this young man. Exploded like a watermelon," he would say.

Arnold convinced himself that the kid he shot was just a curious teenager from a nearby village. From then on he referred to himself, as a shooter, a killer, an evil person. In Arnold's life there was before Vietnam and after Vietnam, a similar life for many of the veterans. Little could bring him solace in his life after that second day in in the Marine compound. He said he had a hole in his soul, and he could not share his sorrow with anyone, including me or his war buddies. He felt he needed to bury all his Vietnam memories just to survive.

The second claim he reported for disability would be a scouting expedition out in the jungle where he and his squad turned a corner and there were three NVA soldiers not paying attention to where they were.

"I was on point and gunned all three down in seconds. I looked at the surprise in their eyes. I asked myself, how could they be so careless? Why did I have to do this?"

His third claim was going into a village that had been napalmed. Marines had to go into the village and kill any remaining people, including women, children, elders, and all their livestock. Vietnamese men would usually leave the area when the Marines were coming into their village taking their water buffalo and a few farm tools. Marines were told that everyone in the village were VC. Raping women was a common occurrence before the soldiers shot the young women.

"One young Vietnamese girl came up to me with pleading in her eyes," Arnold recalled, *"and she whispered... please. I could do nothing. I did not shoot her, but the look in her eyes will never leave me."*

Arnold would not kill anyone on these missions, but he did have to pose the corpses and take pictures of them to send to the Psyop Headquarters for the making of propaganda brochures.

Lastly, and the most horrific act for Arnold was his team patrolling an area when they saw a four or five year old girl set up as a suicide bomber. The NVA told her to run to the American soldiers. Arnold said there was utter silence, but as she came closer, he shot her and blew up the grenades. He would never forgive himself.

He would say, "How could I shoot her and the others in the squad could not. I am truly evil."

His squad would respond, "You were the squad leader. It was your job to protect us, and that is just what you had to do. Don't blame yourself for the predicaments you were in. Blame the U.S. government."

Saving Lives

Though Arnold continued to believe he was evil, he began looking for more ways to save lives. He continued practicing his sniper skills, and if he was at close range, which became more and more common as the NVA knew if they were close to American soldiers, planes and helicopters would not shoot artillery, but Arnold could shoot the fingers and hands off NVA soldiers when at close range. He could maim them, but he would no longer take their lives.

Arnold, at the end of his last tour, decided to die. He thought he could not stand another fire fight. He would just stand up and be killed. His torture would be over. He didn't do it. He was disappointed in himself, but also realized he did want to live. I told him many times, you wanted to live and you did. There is no shame in that.

I tried talking to Arnold about his severe guilt about shooting the Vietnamese. I told him the story of Sofie's Choice, the book by William Styron who questions how much of our lives are determined by us and how much of life is fate. Sofie, the main character in the book is in a German concentration camp and is told by a soldier that he is going to kill one of her two children. He makes her pick which child. Fate can be beyond our comprehension, and we often have no good choices at all. Reacting to fate to save our own lives and others does not make us evil. It makes us human.

Arnold always thought of the other American soldiers he worked with. There was a soldier in his team who seemed to have severe mental health issues. Arnold knew he had no chance of living through the war. Arnold told the young man to stop taking his malaria pills. He told the guy he would get very sick, but it was his ticket home. The soldier did this, he did get sick, and he did get home safe and sound. As Allan would comment, "He didn't go home in a body bag".

Arnold also occasionally observed race riots in the compound between white and black soldiers killing each other. In camp they fought. In fire fights, they were brothers. Those killed in the Marine Compound were reported as shot by enemy fire. He also knew of commanders being killed when they made unreasonable demands and put our soldiers at too high a risk of being killed.

Arnold would say, these young commanders had no war skills and would order their teams into very risky situations. Many of these commanders were killed by their own men.

Arnold began to take his squad away from the most dangerous fire fights.

I could not put my squad in extreme danger when I thought the fire fights we would encounter would end in the death of all of us. The Marines seemed not to care about their choice not to go into battle; And who knew where the Marines were taking their squads?

A most upsetting command that Arnold and his friend Allan received was to put together propaganda brochures offering children $40 to pick up and return unexploded ordinance. Arnold and Allan were appalled. They knew approaching the commander's ethical and moral standards would not succeed in stopping this program, so they brought the commander a budget for the new program. The Army would need to supply small body bags and small caskets for the children who would be killed when the ordinance exploded. The expense would be too much and the commander fell for it. The program was cancelled. What more harm could the U.S. military do to the Vietnamese people?

On April 2, 1970 Arnold received a bronze star for his work with the villages. He did not want it, and when the medal was stolen from our house a couple of years ago, he said he was glad. It meant nothing to him. I am in the process of ordering a new bronze star, and to me, it will represent the lives he saved.

Arnold took two R and R breaks in Bangkok, Thailand. It was a true relief for him. He was amazed by the beautiful city and enjoyed having a break from war. The hotels in Bangkok came with or without a prostitute. Arnold took the "with" option. He was with this girl on both trips. Toy Noi was a beautiful young woman, and I thank her for her caring and compassion for him. He was occasionally in touch with her during his second tour. Arnold sometimes thought that because he was evil, no American girl would marry him, and he thought about marrying an Asian girl. They would understand him.

PART 3

Chapter 11

COMING HOME

Allan's experience

I flew into Oakland at the end of my tour to a sign that said in part, Welcome Home. They had steaks for us and lots and lots of fixings. You could eat your fill, enjoy the United States soil, sit there by yourself and contemplate what had just happened and what it all meant and just what the hell you were going to do next.

We were eventually taken back by random shuttle to the Oakland Army Base for out processing or reassignment depending on how much of your time in the service remained. You know, it was as always, one guy, his duffle bag, and visions or memories. This time it was memories, and that was a big change.

You did not know if the magic BBs (artillery shells) were meant for you during your tour. You lived in the present with hope for a tomorrow. Now, you had to deal with the past. But, I have to say that at that time, the present was pretty damned good. Yeah, you could taste the isolation of everybody, and nobody talked much. But you were alive, you were heading home. For me that was good. I can't speak for any of the others, but I remember thinking about the future. The memories would come back to you soon enough.

But that day was a good day. No drill sergeants, no shipping orders, no night flares or patrols or helicopter pads, no commanding officer or gunny. It was you on the way out of a door you could not see, but you could feel. It was a staggering relief as you stood in the lines and contemplated home.

Arnold's Return – The Letter

While reading through some letters Arnold had sent to his family and one from the Army, I found an unusual letter from the Department of the Army, B Company, 7th Psychological Operations Battalion, San Francisco. After reading it multiple times, I believe the letter was fake. However, whoever wrote it had insight into the war and veteran's suffering from PTSD. This letter arrived at his parents' house shortly before he came home in 1969. The letter is here for all to decide what the meaning of it is.

Issued in solemn warning this twenty-fifth day of March, 1969 to family, friends and neighbors and acquaintances of Arnold B. Bondley.

Very soon, the above named individual will once again be in your midst, de-Americanized, and demoralized; but ready to take his place once again as a human being with freedom, justice, liberty and the somewhat belated pursuit of happiness.

In making your joyous preparation to welcome him back into respectable society, you must make allowance for the crude environment in which he has suffered for the past 12-months. In a sense, he may be a bit vulgar, uncouth, and suffering from downstairs profanity. Remember he must be handled with care.

Therefore, show no alarm if he cringes in terror at the sound of a youngster's toy gun. He might prefer to squat rather than sit in a chair. He will pick at his food suspiciously as if you were trying to poison him.

This was a constant issue with Arnold and I. There were few foods he would eat, and he would want to know what ingredients were in each dish I cooked. He was polite when we had dinner with friends and family, but would ask me when we got home what I thought were in the dishes we ate.

Don't be surprised if he answers all questions with "I hate this place". "It is boring." He may refer to incidences in Vietnam as NUMBA one or NUMBA ten, rating an experience and how he handled it. He may accuse people of being thieves and will carry a gun and knife for protection. He will feel uncomfortable eating in restaurants if he cannot see the entry way. There are few stores he will visit. They feel too confining.

We used to go to concerts in our early marriage, but that soon ended as he gradually became more and more fearful of crowds.

Any of the following sights should be avoided as they can produce an advanced state of shock: people dancing, television, movies, even American women. In a relatively short time, his profanity will decrease enough to permit him to be with a mixed group of people. He may complain of sleeping problems, feeling that he always need to be on guard.

Arnold never slept well. He kept lights on throughout the house every night. He had a gun by his bed. He needed to see what was going on in our house at all times.

> *Make no flattering remarks about exotic southeast Asia. Avoid mentioning the benefits of oversees duty, seasonal weather and don't mention the food. And above all do not mention anything about the so called benefits of RE-EN-LISTING. The reference to these particular subjects may trigger a display of violence.*
>
> *Be especially watchful when he is in the company of women. He may sit and stare. His intentions with women are and will be sincere.*
>
> *Keep in mind that beneath his tanned and rugged exterior there beats a heart of gold. Treasure this, for it is the only thing of value he has left. Treat him with kindness and help him to rehabilitate that which is now the hollow shell of a once proud civilian.*

There was no signature on the letter.

Arnold returned to the states in June of 1970. He came through the San Francisco Airport and was immediately spit on by a civilian and called a baby killer. Arnold quickly changed into civilian clothes. He would never again wear his uniform in public. At the San Francisco air base, going thorough processing, he was asked if he wanted psychological counseling. He said "no". He just wanted to be away from the Army hoping to forget the past two years of this life. He did a good job of this for a while, and he hid it well. It would take 40 years for his PTSD to sneak back into his psyche and for it to become unbearable and unforgettable.

Arnold enrolled at Portland Community College with a new major of architecture the summer of 1970. This is where we met. I was 18 years old. He was 22. I first saw him in a math class. He was an incredibly ruggedly handsome man, tall and strong, soldier strong and so very good looking. He had a big smile that would just take you in. A friend would tease him that he could be the poster boy for Crest toothpaste. The perfect beauty of him was the intelligence and strength that radiated from him. His presence so was striking. As I got to know him, I would see just how smart, driven, kind, and honest he was. I knew the first day I saw him, he would be my husband, the love of my life. Yes, I do believe in love at first sight. It took some convincing for him to fall for me. It may not have been love at first sight for him, but there certainly was lust.

After observing him for a few days, I knew I had to meet him, but he seldom came to class. He did not have to. He was so smart. I knew we had a test one Friday, and he would have to come to class, so I got all dolled up. I was wearing my pink wool pencil skirt with a slit up the back, my pink mohair sweater, cream colored heels and matching pearl necklace and earrings. I got his attention. We had coffee that afternoon and had a dinner date set up for the weekend.

Shortly, before he died he asked me if I remembered what I wore the first time we met, 47 years earlier, and I said "you bet". I knew for sure then that I really had got his attention, and he still remembered me as that 18 year old girl.

Arnold told me immediately after we met, he was a Vietnam veteran. He also told me he did not want a wife. He did not want to love anyone or care for anyone. He did not trust anyone. I knew differently, and I would prove it to him. He could trust me with all his secrets and fears, ALWAYS. I would never betray him.

Under that masculine bravado, there was a man who was hurt and vulnerable. I loved the combination of who he was, strong and caring, yet sometimes frightened with the thoughts of war. I knew he would love me and would care for me. And, I would do the same for him. His first words to me, I did not believe, and Arnold would come around to see that what we had would last for a lifetime. He always had my back, and I had his.

Arnold and I were engaged in March of 1971 and married in June. When I promised to love and honor him, I had to make a secret promise to Arnold that I would never tell anyone he was in Vietnam. At that time, I did not know what he had experienced overseas. It would take him 35 years to begin to open up to me. But, I took this pledge seriously until 2009 when his PTSD would roar its ugly head and made it impossible for me to keep his secrets anymore.

Chapter 12

HOW I THOUGHT
OF OUR MARRIAGE

I have always admired Jackie Kennedy, her demeanor, her acceptance and her belief that she and her husband had a short time of living in Camelot, and I have always felt the same about Arnold and I. We had our Camelot too. Marriage to me was summoning the strength to go the duration always moving forward toward the unknown with courage and a belief in what our lives could be. Arnold's life was like a mosaic to me, a beautiful conversation between what was broken and what could be repaired. Look closely at a mosaic and you will see the broken pieces. Stand away and you will see beauty.

Terry Tempest Wills wrote, "Is our love an illusion, or is it when our eyes meet and we know our love is true?" Our love was no illusion, it was truth through and through. Our mosaic was real, broken yet beautiful. I remember waking up the day after we were married, looking at Arnold and thinking, I can hardly believe this man is my husband. He was mine and is mine for all eternity.

Karen and Arnold's Marriage, 1971

Chapter 13

OUR LIVES BEGIN

Arnold would finish out his degree at the University of Oregon. He loved school and did well. His only blip was a D grade he would receive for supposedly cheating and plagiarizing on a design contest. Not true. He was an excellent designer. But, it hurt him. Another kick in the gut, not being trusted, not being able to trust.

Arnold graduated in 1974. His first job was with the City of Portland. He was there less than a year, as he did not like the bureaucracy of a government agency. He would no longer take orders from anyone. Our God son Ed, a carpenter, said, he always enjoyed working with Vietnam Vets because of their independence and unwillingness to take orders. "They did things their way," he would say. That was certainly Arnold's way.

Arnold did win a national award for one of his buildings, the first all gender, individual restrooms in the country. They were designed to look like pier poles. These buildings are located at Willamette Park on the river in Portland. He always laughed about that. But, I think he was a leader in the 70's in architectural gender equality. When he quit working for the city, he worked for a local architect to finish his two years of internship designing restaurants, homes, clinics, and clothing stores.

After he finished his internship, we went to Europe and stayed in France for five weeks with college friends. We drove their tiny two cylinder car and stayed with their friends and relatives. We had so much fun and felt so welcomed.

A party in France

The French have still not forgotten World War II and how U.S. involvement led to their liberation. Our friend Andre Pierre had been in the French military and knew about Vietnam. I think his caring for Arnold's experience helped steel their friendship.

Travel would become a saving grace for both of us. We both loved to experience new places and new people and the beauty of the countries we visited. Travel would become our escape. It seemed Vietnam could not find us when we left the U.S.

Chapter 14

DEALING WITH PTSD AT HOME

When we returned from France, Arnold felt free to move on with his life, a life he chose, a life he controlled. He set up an architectural practice and a construction business. He wanted to forget Vietnam, and it seemed to me he had most of the time.

I truly believe that his choice of career helped to save him during this time. Because he chose architecture, building, and art as a career, he was able to create. He was no longer destroying.

There were occasions however when he used drugs and would leave home for a few days to a week hanging out with friends. I think these were reality breaks from the new world he lived in. Vietnam seemed to call him at these times. Sometimes at home he would be staring (the 1000 yard stare as soldiers call it). I would ask him where are you? And he would say, "Leave me alone" or "I wish I could go back to Vietnam for one more fire fight. There is nothing like surviving a fire fight. I'd stand up after the fight and try to figure out if I was alive or dead. Then I'd head back to the compound and pretend it never happened. Life in the states is boring. I have no real purpose." Thinking about how to stay alive, he no longer needed to do, but at times he could not let go of those thoughts.

Other ways of dealing with PTSD episodes was driving fast cars, boating (launching his little fishing boat into the air by driving over floating logs), driving motorcycles, mountain climbing, and flying planes (he liked to do stunt flying). He liked anything that was risky. I remember him taking me in a small plane into the crater of Mt. St. Helens in Washington. I have never been so scared. I thought we would crash for sure as we circled down into the crater. But he pulled the plane up just as we were getting close to the ground. I continued to fly with him as I became a little of a risk taker myself, and he didn't do anything too wild again with me. When I was not with him and he was coming in for a landing, he would fly low over our house and tip the plane wing. I knew he had had a good flight and was feeling exhilarated.

The 80s

I was very lucky to be best friends with one of Arnold's war buddies Steve's wife Sheri. She took things more in stride, or so it seemed to me, and we would talk on the phone when Arnold would take off. She seemed to believe that fate was fate and our guys would find a way to survive, or they wouldn't. She seemed better at accepting this than I did. But thank goodness she has always been there for me and continues to help guide me through my grief of losing Arnold.

Flying to Mexico 1982

Climbing Mt Rainer Washington 1985

Chapter 15

HAPPY TIMES

In 1974, shortly before we left for Europe, we bought our first house. A Victorian in an old neighborhood of Portland. It needed lots of work, and we worked on the house most nights and weekends. There were more young couples moving into the area, many of them veterans. All of us working to create new happy lives. We had many parties and enjoyed our new happy carefree life immensely. Other week ends we would visit our friends Steve and Sheri.

Steve was in Vietnam the same time as Arnold and fairly close to Freedom Hill at Phu Bai. He and Arnold were in Fort Lewis, Washington for a couple of months before being discharged. They were hellions and loved to tell Sheri and I about their escapades. Evenings were spent at the base movie theater and looking for pretty women at the local bars. They claim they never found them! One of their favorite tricks was to take pie pans from the kitchen and put them in the big clothes dryers in the basement of their living quarters at night. That got everyone up. They would also lock themselves inside their rooms so they did not have to get up early, 6:00 am to salute the flag. Arnold would never again salute the flag he no longer cared about. Roommate Steve just liked to sleep in. The flag to him remains sacred.

Arnold and Steve went into a construction business together in the mid-70s. Arnold designed and helped build. Steve and his brother Mark built some beautiful homes including ours. Sheri and I were painters. We also bought an insulation machine, painted our old VW bus in rainbow colors and worked around the city insulating the attics and walls of older houses and apartments. It was a popular business then, and we did well. It was at a time when energy prices were skyrocketing and homeowners wanted warmer houses and lower utility bills. Arnold was good at predicting needs when it came to economics.

Our other joy was becoming God parents to Steve and Sheri's two young children, Ed and Jenny. In later years both of these young people would help us build our house on the coast. I remain close to both of these young people, and enjoy spending time with them and their three children.

In the early 1980s, Arnold and I bought a couple of acres of land just outside Portland in a rural wooded area butting up to a 5000 acre natural park. Phase two of our lives were beginning. Now our summer and fall evenings involved preparing to build. We dug out the foundation, put in electricity, water, a septic system and carved out a road to our property. It took us two years to sell our Victorian home but when we did, we put up a large tent on our property and built a storage shed, where we kept our tools and refrigerator and slept during stormy weather, and of course we built an outhouse. It was the most fun summer we could have imagined. Our friends Steve and brother Mark would come up the gravel road behind the house every morning, honking their horn. It was our alarm. All three men began building the house and stayed for nearly six months. By November 1st of 1982, the 3000 square foot house was closed in and we moved out of the tent into the downstairs art studio. We insulated it, put in a wood stove and completed one bathroom. It was still really cold but we pushed on with wiring and plumbing. In the spring, we sheet rocked and painted and moved upstairs. I shingled the outside of the house. It would take us another three years to fully complete the house. We lived there in the beautiful woods for ten years.

Arnold and Steve continued to work on smaller jobs now because the economy was doing poorly, and the need for architectural work dwindled for Arnold. I went to work as a secretary for a nearby hospital, taking classes at Portland State University. I realized that both of us needed a good career that would pay us enough to live the lifestyle we wanted. I majored in sociology thinking I would become a social worker. The hospital and my Dad helped pay my way through school. I was following my Dad's advice of learning to take care of myself and not depend on others. I think I was successful with that goal.

While money was tight when I was in school, we continued to have a lot of fun. We started cross country skiing with our friends and continued traveling. Some of our favorite trips were to local hot springs. There are many hot springs in the Cascade Mountain range east of Portland. We often took our God son Ed with us. He was about eight years old, and he would say, "Why would you pay to take a bath?" Ed always kept us laughing. Our friendship with

Steve and Sheri continued to grow and other weekends became our time to party and party we did. Our favorite beverage was cheap apricot and boysenberry wine. We joke about that still.

As the economy continued to slow down both Arnold and I knew we could not afford such a large house and the taxes that went along with it. During a weekend trip to the coast in 1991, Arnold said, "Let's sell the house, move to the coast and build a small spec house, and you can finish school." I didn't want to go at first as I thought there were no job opportunities at the coast, which survives on fishing, timber harvests, and tourism. I was a city girl. But, I capitulated. Why not have another building adventure? Living in the outdoors and building a house are some of my best memories, and I know Arnold was proud of the houses he, Mark, Steve and Ed built for us.

When we got home on Monday, Arnold hired a Realtor. Two days later the house was sold for twice what we had anticipated. We had sixty days to move.

We bought a used travel trailer to live in. Every day we looked at ocean view lots from Astoria to Newport, Oregon. We found one quickly, a double, flat sized lot, in Lincoln City. We bought it on contract. Then we headed home and started packing with the help of Ed. We rented two storage units and pretty much tossed everything in. Our last day there, Arnold filled his truck with tools, hooked his boat up with more tools and took our dog. I filled my car with camping supplies and took our cat. We arrived in the evening of that last day in June, and it was so strange. The trailer had been delivered a few days before to the building lot. We had no electricity or water. It was raining and cold on that June night. I felt really lost and strange and wondered what the heck I had been talked into. But, the next day, the sun came out, and our new neighbor sent over a water hose and an electric line. Ed showed up shortly after and worked with us during his college vacation. His sister, Jenny came later to help us insulate. Our good friend Mark also showed up with his trailer, and we began the build. This 1400 sq. ft. house was a 2 ½ story home with an ocean view from the top floor where our living space was located. On the second floor there were two large bedrooms and a bath. Both of these bedrooms would be used as studio space. We also built an oversized double garage to work as a shop and a decent size family room, which we never finished as we learned to live in small quarters just fine. While we loved our new home, it proved to be a real challenge when Arnold became ill, as it was not at all disability friendly, and it was not the house that would work well for Arnold after he became paralyzed.

However, because of the small size of the house and our work, we were able to pay the house and land off within two years. Our house goal was met. No house payments by the time we were 40. We did it. Freedom! More money to travel and to be with friends, all Vietnam vets and their wives. There seemed to be no stress when we were with these friends. The guys understood each other as did the wives. I feel so lucky to have found friends who would sustain us through good times and bad. These friends continue to support me in my grief of losing Arnold, and we continue to travel together.

I traveled to Portland two days a week in 1991 for school and finished my degree in six months. And, the job situation was much different than we had anticipated. The economy was picking up as a large number of Californians were moving to the

Oregon coast because it was fairly cheap living here and the climate was mild.

Arnold had work before we even finished our house. He was the only architect in our town. And, he no longer needed to do construction work. He designed restaurants and houses, all of them hanging off the beautiful rock cliffs over the Pacific ocean. One of his projects, Tidal Raves Restaurant, was used in a Hollywood movie called Burning Plain. We both thought that was quite an honor, and Arnold was able to watch a lot of the filming. It didn't win an academy award, but I thought Arnold had. It was important to me that Arnold was proud of his creations. It helped his PTSD.

I went to work for our local community hospital. I was lucky to be able to do many different jobs. At first, I recruited physicians and nurses. Then I took over the public relations office, and began writing grants and contracts. In later years, I would work for Oregon Health and Science University as an outreach worker teaching health career classes to rural high school students. At this same time, our friends Steve and Sheri moved to eastern Washington for Steve's job, as he was now a railroad engineer and Sheri completed her college degree and opened a disabilities business. We were far away from each other, but we never lost our love and friendship for these two wonderful people and their children. Our God children grew up, married and had children. We now had five wonderful people in our lives, and we all could afford a little more than fruit wine when we got together.

Because we were so far from each other, we began taking trips to spend time with all the Cousineau family, Steve, Sheri and their children, spending time in eastern and western Oregon and

Washington, and even Canada, continuing taking trips to numerous hot springs. Steve and Sheri still do that today. We went to Hawaii. We started taking cruises to Europe, the Caribbean, and Central America. These were our absolute best times. Arnold and I managed at least three trips a year. I am so glad that we traveled our entire married life instead of waiting until retirement, camping when we were young and cruising as we got older.

The Middle Years

Arnold and I had some very good times, even a good life, living in Portland and for the last 26 years, in Lincoln City, Oregon on the coast. Arnold really loved the coast. He loved the raging storms we would have. He called coast weather "real weather."

Arnold went on to build a successful architectural practice. I went on to get degrees in marketing, and corporate communications. I continued my work at our local hospital on the Oregon coast as a technical writer and health careers teacher. We both had very successful and rewarding careers. We were always busy. This helped us find happiness. We felt good about our work, friendships and family. I think this life kept Arnold's PTSD at bay.

Because Arnold had his PTSD issues around the killing of the child in Vietnam, we decided not to have children. He felt he did not deserve that happiness. By the time the issue of children came up, we had been married 12 years, and I had some fertility issues. It seemed to me, it was fate that had chosen a different life for us.

We started traveling a lot more, back to Europe, Central America, Mexico, Caribbean, Canada, and lots of travel in the western U.S. and Hawaii. Though we lived on the rainy Oregon coast, we both loved the desert of eastern Oregon, Washington and SW states. We usually spent a couple of weeks each year in the eastern deserts or Hawaii during the winter when Oregon was drenched in rain. It was always good to find some sunshine. Travel would lift our spirits in the winter and help us make it to the beautiful summers we would experience on the coast.

Our everyday lives were busy. We both worked long hours. We worked hard and we had very specific life goals. We had bought and sold houses, traveled, and had good times with our friends. Arnold retired and I was working just part time. We wanted to live long happy lives with lots of travel. My father was a lot like us. He was an incredible saver. He had grown up during the Depression. He liked Arnold's desire to provide a good life for us. Arnold and my Dad liked playing the stock market, and investing in precious metals. My Dad would sometime give us money to invest in a certain stock. Our friend Steve gave us railroad stock, which I still have. We always did well. Our retirement was well planned, and in early 2012 the next stage of our plan would become reality. We owned our house and cars. We enjoyed our freedom. We then took a long trip to Europe with friends Steve and Sheri. We continued with more happy travels and adventures.

Chapter 16

THE HARD TIMES BEGIN

In 2009, Arnold seemed to be more bothered by PTSD as did his friend Steve. He had difficulty finishing the house he was designing. He would sit for hours in front of his drafting table and computer. He did manage to finish the project, but we decided it was time for him to retire. He was 62 and was eligible for social security and had a decent pension. Steve felt it would be good for him to work on his PTSD issues as he had done a few years before. I wanted Arnold to feel peace which he did not feel at this time.

Arnold was in PTSD therapy for three years. He did CBT (Cognitive Behavioral Therapy) a therapy that takes you back to your trauma and slowly brings you home where you could start to believe that the trauma was truly over and that you were safely home. Unfortunately, this therapy did not work for Arnold. He never believed he was safe, and he thought he and I were in danger all the time. He began telling me the CIA was spying on us. He did not want me to use the phone as he thought it was being tapped. He carried a gun and knife at all times. He hated for me to be gone, and I did have to travel some for my job. He would always have excuses as to why it would not be safe for me to be on a plane and to stay in a strange hotel in a strange city. My car was always in tip top shape. He was always fearful that I would have a break down. Having car trouble worried him. He made sure I carried a pistol when traveling.

During therapy, he became even more interested in guns and knives. He had a conceal permit and always carried a gun in his truck. At home, he drove his pickup to places unknown to me, most likely up on the Siletz River. Nature helped calm him down. If I asked where he had been for the last four hours, he would say getting a cup of coffee. One day that story was actually true, as our local coffee shop owner called me in the afternoon to say Arnold had ordered 23 cups of coffee that day, and they were very worried about him. When I confronted him when he returned that evening, he denied he had done that. His mental status was declining. I thought it was PTSD which was there, but I would later find out that he had also been diagnosed with early dementia a more and more common disease among PTSD Vietnam veterans.

In January 2012, I was fired from my hospital job a few months before I had planned to retire to spend more time with Arnold. I knew then he was not well. My firing was not terribly upsetting to me as I planned to retire that summer. For Arnold, I had been disrespected, and he went into full blown PTSD, preparing his guns and knives. He believed he was in Vietnam, and he had decided he was going to go on a killing spree. I would later learn after his death, he was targeting a group of people I knew. I would find this information in his journal, and I was surprised at the depth of his intentions. This was a very hard time for me. Arnold had talked of killing in the past, and I had always been able to talk him down from his destructive plans fairly quickly. Now he remained in the planning mode. I still thought it would pass.

Arnold took off in his pickup one day, very upset. Luckily, he was driving away from where the the city was located. I did not know if he had weapons, though I knew it was likely. In general I felt very uncomfortable. I felt I had to get in touch with the VA suicide hotline immediately. I called the hotline, and they asked me if Arnold had his cell phone. I said "yes." Within minutes his personal psychologist had got in touch with him, and had convinced him to admit himself to the VA psych unit. He came home and off we went. I am so thankful for the VA's quick response to our crisis.

At the VA hospital, Arnold had an eight hour intake. He was convinced he and I were in Vietnam, and we were going to set up a trap for the people we would kill. He was then placed in lock down and was there for a week. He refused to see me as he felt I had betrayed him by calling the VA, although he did visit with our God daughter, Jenny and my cousin Brittany. These two young women always helped him calm down. It would be new medications that brought him back home to me.

When we did get home, he slept for nearly a week, heavily sedated. He and I made it through another trauma, this time at home. And, I had a new part time job working with 4H teaching after school science to elementary students. It was a wonderful job, and I worked it until Arnold became severally ill.

For the next year, Arnold stayed by himself in his studio designing brick structures for our backyard including a pizza oven and fireplace and paths throughout the property. I sometimes wondered if he would brick over the entire yard. He loved this kind of work, and he could be alone working outdoors. He began the work the following fall.

At this time, he seldom spoke to me. He put up a wall of silence. I felt lonely and scared. He was slipping away from me, and I didn't know what to do, so I did nothing, hoping for recovery. I don't know if that was a mistake or not. What could I have done? His PTSD was worsening, and I felt more therapy would not help him. In the past, it had made him worse. I began to think that he could not live much longer with his Vietnam flashbacks that would not recede. I began to think that death was his only escape, and I thought he was thinking that too.

Arnold now seldom slept or ate. He would work in our yard day and night even when it was poring down rain. He set up lights at night to work. If I tried to talk to him, he would physically push me away and leave in his truck. He was stuck. I was stuck, both of us spiritually stranded. I knew he loved me, and I loved him, but he just couldn't be around anyone including me. He stopped all contact with Allan and had little contact with Steve. Luckily, he did have some contact with our two cousins, Brittany and Julie. Both girls had experienced trauma in their childhoods and could relate to Arnold's trauma, maybe better than I could.

He did finally agree to see his primary care doctor in Salem who told him he was in good health. At least, that is what Arnold told me. I found out after he died that he had been diagnosed with severe PTSD and early stage dementia. During this time, Arnold continued his same behavior. He continued to eat very little. He lived on Pepsi, coffee, chocolate milk, and toast. When he was admitted to the hospital in 2015, he was diagnosed with malnutrition.

Yet, we continued on. I believed he was close to death. I was guessing a stroke or heart attack would take him from me, and there was nothing I could do. He had medications, but often refused or forgot to take them. I even began to feel prepared for his death. I would find out later, I was not at all prepared. But, it was his life, to choose to try to get well or die. I knew he was choosing death. Though I thought he was close to dying, I did not expect something in between with two years of severe illness and disability.

Chapter 17

THE LAST TWO YEARS

On May 17, 2015, Arnold came into the house and told me he thought he was having a heart attack. He took an aspirin, and said he as going to lay down. I talked him into letting me take him to our local ER. I will always wonder if I should have let him go then, on his terms. There would be multiple times when I could have chosen this for him, but I just couldn't let him go. Was I a coward? Was I forcing him to live when he didn't want to? I still can't answer that question today.

The local physicians at the hospital said he was not having a heart attack, but had the beginnings of heart failure. I breathed a sigh of relief. My Dad had heart failure and lived for three years. I thought this might be a wake up call for Arnold to take better care of himself. I headed home that evening feeling fairly relieved and even hopeful.

When I returned in the morning, Arnold had taken a turn for the worse. His heart was encased in fluid making it very hard for it to beat normally. Our local doctors could not get his pulse rate and blood pressure up to anywhere near normal. The VA sent a trauma team by ambulance to take him to the Portland VA ICU. He would spend seven weeks in the hospital where he had four strokes, two head and two spinal cord, and he spent a week on life support. He whispered to me on his first day at the VA hospital, "Don't let me die". I complied. I did not follow his advance directives, and again I will always wonder if that was the right thing to do. But, he said he wanted to live, and I would help him fight for his life. His cardiologist said he was such a strong guy, he thought he had a chance, only a 1 percent chance of living, and he would not likely live for more than a year. In reality, he lived for two years, not a happy or easy life, but a life. The spinal cord strokes would paralyze him from his chest down. He now had his arms, hands, shoulders, and head that he could move. This was extremely upsetting to him. He was very fearful, something I had never seen in him. He could no longer take care of us, protect us anymore.

One day he said to me after we returned home, "My short term memory is gone. What are we going to do?" I said, "We will use my short term memory." I think it is in pretty good shape." But he now had a gun and knives next to his bed remaining in his fearful state all the time. His bed was set up in the laundry room, the only room without stairs and where he could see both the front and back door. We left all the house lights on at all times. As our house had been robbed while he was in the hospital. Arnold felt very vulnerable that it would happen again, even though the youth who robbed us were now in prison.

After seven weeks at the Portland VA, most of that time spent in the ICU, he was transferred to the Puget Sound VA in Seattle to the spinal cord unit (SCI) where he would remain for over ten months in physical and cardiac therapy. His depression was severe. He had memory loss which could have been caused by the strokes or the worsening dementia. He had left and right neglect, which made him only look forward. He said he could see side-to-side but he seldom moved his head. Some nurses told me that this type of neglect could result in him only seeing black when he did turn his head. Arnold was devastated he would never drive again. He took the test two times and failed both. He was at high risk for suicide, so I learned from his medical notes after he died, but I was never told that when he was in the hospital. I am guessing Arnold did not want me or anyone to know.

Coming Home from the Hospital

We came home in early 2016. Arnold was bedridden and was very fearful of using his wheelchair. He did do some exercises with a physical therapist, but when she stopped her work with him, his depression increased and he refused to do his exercises. As he had fallen out of bed a few times, he also feared falling out of the wheelchair. The portable lifts the VA gave us were too short to lift Arnold anywhere.

He had gained weight and any kind of movement was difficult. He spent his days reading (he now liked to read the classics and philosophy). This was very different for him as he had always enjoyed technical writing and reading. He watched a lot of television. I bought him three baby chicks to care for and he seemed to enjoy spending time with them. Chickens were his favorite pet, and we had adult hens until I gave them away when we were in Seattle for his therapy. The new chicks would sit on his chest and watch TV. Those chickens still like to watch TV with me.

The few times Arnold went outside, the chicks would ride on his power chair with him. Our cats seemed frightened of Arnold. I think it was due to the noise his air bed motor made. I felt bad about that as Arnold loved our new kitten Riley. I could not turn the bed off because it would be flat and hard and Arnold had issues with pressure sores. Pressure sores can be deadly, and we could not afford for him to have anymore health issues. It was usual for Arnold to get a bladder infection and a new foot sore every month he was home. Luckily, the VA let him receive treatment at our local hospital. I'm sure the staff at the hospital called Arnold a frequent flyer, but I think they all cared for him a great deal. We had home nursing services six days a week and physician services every month. I received payment for caring for Arnold and had house cleaning services too and eight hours a week of respite care. The VA payed my brother-in-law, Dennis to care for him on those days. That would have been helpful, but an hour after I left to run errands I would get a call from Arnold asking me to come home. He really wanted me with him 24/7. I belonged to a VA spinal cord support group, and many of the wives I spoke with had the same issues, their husbands wanting their wives to be with them all the time. One vet had cameras set up in his house so he could see his wife where ever she was. It was tough times for all of us.

In-home care from the VA was exceptional. I had a social worker assigned to me. She helped me with a new disability application. When Arnold died she worked with me to obtain a DCI pension for combat widows and widowers, and she continues to help me work through the disability process which is now going on two years of work. She helped me become Arnold's representative, and I now am eligible for a variety of VA benefits including two years of back disability pay, housing, health care, and education. I would like all veteran widows and widowers to know of these services because I am sure many of them do not. VA social workers are located at all VA clinics and can be a godsend when you have so much going on with caring for your veteran and dealing with their death. Families can also meet with a Veterans Service Officer located in all counties in the U.S.

Arnold lived at home for a little over a year. It was not a good life. He was bedridden and was very fearful of falling out of bed and out of of his his wheelchair. Although strapped into the chair, he always feared falling. I gave up taking him on walks, as his fear was intolerable, and the walks became too difficult for me to deal with. There was just no way for me to convince him he was safe in any situation.

Of all things, a dentist appointment would make Arnold's desire to die known to me. It was January 2nd, 2017. He took a heavy fall trying to get into the wheelchair. I called EMTs to get him back into bed. That night Arnold told me simply "I'm done." I thought he meant, with the wheelchair, and I didn't pay much attention to what he said. He was upset. Later that evening he called me from upstairs and told me there was more. He was done living, no more hospitalizations, no more doctor or nurse visits. "I won't use a gun," he said. "I will not do that to you." He told me not to be afraid. He had seen the white light in the hospital, and that is where he wanted to go. I asked if he would continue taking his medications. He said he would. At that time, I still did not know if he was serious, as daily life continued on for us.

There were no changes in his health. No more talk of death. Though in poor health, he was stable. However, I did find out later he had begun planning his death in early December 2016. He was reviewing our bank accounts and pension plans. He bought four necklaces in early December from Amazon. One for his sister, one for me and one for each of our cousins. He bought me a four leaf clover. He joked that I would need luck in the near future. From then on, he ate little, and sipped ice water to help quench his thirst. His last meal was two teaspoons of mashed potatoes three days before he died. Dehydration and kidney fail-ure would take his life.

On January 26th, he began to go into a delirium. He was in terrible pain. I suspected he had a bladder infection. His body was very cool to the touch. I did not know that his body was shutting down. I asked him to take the antibiotics we always had on hand. He said "no". I asked him to go to the hospital. He said "no". His pain was worsening. He kept telling me not to be afraid. When someone you live with is in such misery you don't know what to hope for, death or more of same with a slim chance of some recovery. None of the choices were good. I thought, let fate make the decision. Fate had made a lot of his decisions throughout his life. I think Arnold believed he needed to suffer pain, just as he had inflicted pain on the Vietnamese and saw his dying buddies suffer. He called out their names as he started his journey out of this world. Arnold went boldly into war and boldly to his death. He was so brave and determined to die on his own terms.

I really wanted to call a nurse to get him on hospice, but I was afraid they would hospitalize him and put him in their psyche ward, and I knew he did not want that. He wanted to die at home. By the 27th, he became more delirious. Again I asked him to go to the hospital as he was in so much pain. He said "no". I thought he was close to death. But he made it to the next day. I did increase his pain meds those last days. It is all I could do to help.

I had forgotten that his bathing aid, Cheryl would come on Monday the 28th. Arnold was no longer coherent. Cheryl took one look at him when she arrived and called 911. I didn't know what to do. So off we went. As we left, Cheryl said to Arnold "Don't you die on me!" She cared about him so much as did all his nurses. At the ER, he was in terrible pain, but because he could barely breath, the doctor did not want him heavily sedated. Arnold was admitted to the hospital at three o'clock in the afternoon. He was put on life support at six as he had signed a resuscitate order in the fall of 2016.

At our local hospital, an ambulance was called to take Arnold to the Samaritan Corvallis Hospital, the closest trauma hospital to the coast. I went home and put a few clothes in a suitcase and left for Corvallis. I still had hope. When I got to the ICU, Arnold was not there, and I saw a priest coming toward me. I knew. Arnold had coded two times in the ambulance right after they left Lincoln City, so the crew turned around and brought him back to our community hospital. Arnold had coded another time while in the ER in Lincoln City. He was still alive. I talked to a nurse who said Arnold had gone a significant amount of time without oxygen to his brain. He would likely be in a vegetative state if they could save him. He was semi conscience, and the nurse Sue said she was sure he could hear. She was with him and had been talking to him and she thought he was hearing her. So, I took the phone and told him "I loved him, and it was okay to let go. Find that white light you saw this afternoon and follow it." Arnold died about a half an hour before I got back to the Lincoln City Hospital a little after midnight. He was so cold to the touch. I took his hand and warmed it up and it curled around mine. I felt his soul was still there with me. I kissed him and said my final goodbye.

Arnold had a military honors funeral. 21 gun salute, and taps. My family and friends were a great support to me as were Arnold's war buddies, Steve and Allan and my cousin Pat. The Patriot Motorcycle riders were there. Arnold's' buddies and my cousin saluted him as he was put back in the hearse. I will never forget that gesture. I gave the eulogy. I felt strong and empowered. I talked about agent orange. I wanted everyone to know it was agent orange that took his life. It took over 40 years, but it got him in the end, and I no longer had to keep any of Arnold's secrets. And here they are laid out in this book.

Chapter 18

THE PTSD JOURNAL

I found Arnold's' PTSD journal in his bookcase a few months after his death. It seemed to jump out at me. I felt stunned after I read it. I had a better understanding of his PTSD issues. It also disturbed me that he just could not let go of his Vietnam thoughts. Of course I felt compelled to read it, and I am sure he meant for me to find it. I knew some of what had happened to him in Vietnam, but not to the extent he wrote about. I had no idea what he wanted me to do with the journal. If I published it, I believed I would be helping family, friends, care providers and Vietnam vets; But was I betraying him? Many times, Arnold had told me that when he died, to do what I needed to do to bring myself comfort. Sharing his life with others does bring me comfort. It keeps him alive in my mind. He is alive in this story. I felt a strong need to write this. I hope he can forgive me, if it was not what wanted. I suspect he didn't feel his life was worth telling, but I did, and I do.

Arnold began VA psychological therapy in November of 2009 and would remain in therapy for three years. He tells his therapist that he goes into PTSD mode when someone stands close to him. He does not like being touched. He cannot bring himself to enter a store (Ah, this makes sense to me now. I did all our shopping because he said he did not like to shop). He was fearful of elevators. He could not read or watch movies or television about war. He always said movies about war were not real. You had to experience it, live it, to understand it. He saw and heard way too much in Vietnam. He avoided situations to avoid anxiety. He avoided certain places when he felt he was getting worse, and he worried he would go crazy. He could not listen to 60s music. When his squad was getting ready to leave the Marine compound, not knowing where they were going or for what purpose, they would play music for the hour they were given to get ready for battle. He knew it may be the last music he would ever hear. When driving, he could not stand to be driving behind a car because he could not see what was in front of him. He drove very fast and said he knew he was putting other peoples' lives in jeopardy. He admitted this to his counselor. He would drive 140 miles an hour, yes! His BMW was a sports model, and it had power, and it made him feel powerful. I think it made him feel in control. Control is how he thought he would get rid of his PTSD. He was so wrong. Sometimes fate gets in the way, and we lose control. He needed to let go, to release his mind from the horror of Vietnam. He needed hope for his future, but he never found it those last years of his life. He could not let go of Vietnam.

Smelling certain spices made his PTSD strong. There were many times when Arnold would leave when I was cooking.

I could not determine what spice was bothering him. Was it the smell of cooking meat? In his journal, he says he cannot stand the smell of the sweet, sickening smell of garlic. Ultimately, I realized when the Marines would attack a village, the first thing they would smell would be food cooking, and when combat began, Arnold could smell burning of flesh.

The Vietnam War Defined My Life

At the age of 19, I felt I knew my rights, and I felt able to stand up for them. I was drafted and sent to Vietnam as a shooter, if you will, and was instructed to kill as many VC as possible, the enemy of course, in order to build the body count for the politicians. Body counts were the measure of success for this war. There was no interest in taking land. Apparently most people directing or advocating our involvement thought a high body count meant success. After a fire fight, I and my team would have to take the rifles the NVA had along with wallets, family photos, and uniform insignia. Doubt about our effectiveness permeated the thoughts of many Americans. I arrived just after the North Vietnamese were administering a surprisingly large object lesson in humility. Their TET offensive showed that we could be beaten back in spite of our superior fire power. Field commanders were embarrassed, angry, and trigger happy.

Our job continued to be improving the image of the government of South Vietnam and to help pacify people in the villages and hamlets that were considered sympathetic to the enemy, furnishing manpower and food. We also tried to demoralize the

North Vietnamese troops using the screeching loudspeakers during fire fights, leaflet drops to improve the image of the South Vietnamese and by entertaining the people in marginally sympathetic villages at night. We showed a propaganda film, a cartoon, and always a John Wayne movie using a 16 mm projector with a large canvas screen.

The Journal Questionnaire

Arnold's counselor says, "What is your situation?" Arnold replies, *"I am a shooter, I am 100% a shooter. I am angry a lot. I saw a lot of carnage due to government mandated shooting, and that is a fact. I am not exaggerating. My feelings are based on fact. I can shoot at any time. I'm always ready because the military dictated all my activities. I was told by my country to shoot the enemy. Shoot anything that moves. I'm stuck with these thoughts. Other issues I worry about are safety and trust. Sometimes, I get drunk at home. I hear my wife and I am worried about her. I hope she is not going anywhere."* Lastly, he said, *"I have very low self esteem, no self worth, I'm overly cautious. I self criticize, and I have intimacy issues."*

Arnold told me he suffered from PTSD about 75% of the time. He felt unable to handle anxiety. He said he needed to learn about gaining back power and control in therapy. I think the therapy was meant to help him forgive himself and to live for now and the future, but he was stuck in the past and would remain there until the day he died.

JOURNAL NOTES

My time in Vietnam

My time in Vietnam involved working with the Vietnamese villagers in Quang Nam Province, a key strategic area because of the air base and the million people living in the city of Da Nang. Psyop teams and their interpreters were responsible for providing pro-Vietnam government messages to people with unknown sympathies by means of movies we showed in the villages at night, leaflets dropped by plane or helicopter and loud speakers to scare the enemy and with help to move some Vietnamese women, children, and elders out of harms way. Our responsibilities included documenting atrocities at the aftermath of contact, so photos and specific NVA unit information could be used in leaflets that encouraged surrendering (Chieu Hoi) in a timely manner and stop their threat and keep the failure of their missions fresh in their minds. During cordon and search operations, we used the loudspeakers to coordinate and direct villagers to areas of safety. Though the villagers had their own methods of staying safe with bunkers built under their huts or out in in jungle near their villages.

The incidents of war, such as rocket attacks, sniper harassments and suicide sappers, were shocking at first, and then after about a month in country, seemed more routine. We became de-sensitized to human carnage, the death of men, women and children, bomb damage and attacks on our person. Everyone was a possible NVA. It felt necessary to kill all Vietnamese. You just could not risk trusting anyone.

One area of responsibility was large, and we traveled daily by truck to the areas needing our help. Most of our troops, the Marines, traveled the roads a few times during their tour, and we traveled those roads often, sometimes several times a day. We could not tolerate the very slow convoys. The mine sweeping and clearing could take four hours, where the trip alone and at a fast pace would take 30 minutes. Our trucks were loaded with sand bags on the floor boards, and we sped along aware of the mines and snipers rationalizing the risky travel.

Arnold also stole a jeep in his first tour. The jeep could go very fast and hopefully saved him from the snipers. Arnold loved his jeep, but it was stolen from him right before he was sent home, left to someone else who needed that fast transport.

Since the movies were shown to civilians in various "hot" villages and hamlets and subjected us to continual risk from the time we set out on the dangerous roads to set up the screen, projector, and generator while waiting for darkness, through 2-3 hours of movies, and return late in the night. It was always dangerous, but traveling fast helped us feel safer.

Since we were normally alone, just the two men and a Vietnamese interpreter, we were cautious and always prepared for enemy action in spite of the large assembly of children, sometimes 50-200 kids would come to see the movies. Each team member had an M-16 and a .45 automatic holstered. In the truck we had more, grenades, 2 LAAWS (super caliber American guns), and a .45 caliber machine gun. When working, we had the M-16 in plain sight, and we kept the kids and others a good distance from them. The .45 auto was used to protect the rifles if necessary.

During battles we were constantly aware of the dangers and power of the war. At first these scenes with mutilated bodies and burned out villages were very disturbing. As time went by, all the team members became numb to the war. This took only about a month.

Visions and recollections of so many weapons of war stick in my memory. Carnage and severely wounded people are seen and will not fade. Did I have a good reason to kill people? Other than ones provided by McNamera and LBJ (President Johnson). NO.

My Life is Changed

Capsulizing my life during Vietnam is not simple because at that time everything was new and different. My life was changed, taken over and controlled from the time I was drafted. It was a new life for me fighting with the U.S. Marines in I Corps and realizing this could be my last life stage of life. I figured I may never reach the age when I could legally have a beer or vote. That is not the position I wanted to be in; it was forced upon me, and if I was killed or maimed, our politicians would argue that it was for the glory of the United States. The thought that I could be killed at any moment settled in permanently, and if that is considered a stuck point, I think I will be stuck forever.

Most people I knew in the Vietnam war, doing what I was doing, came to the realization they very likely would be killed or wounded. If you didn't deal with this reality, you could not do your job well. One man in our group was worried so much that *we were able to have him transferred to a clerk position so not put our squad in danger. A soldier who froze in battle put everyone in a very dangerous position. More soldiers were transferred to clerk positions as a way to keep them safe and the combat troops safer.*

Arnold was responsible for these transfers. Every new man who came to his squad was observed by Arnold, and he decided who could and could not take on fire fights and then make the transfers happen if need be.

So my hyper vigilance is not only due to thoughts that some individuals may approach me with a knife, but to a group of people taking responsibility for the country and its people, who might use their authority to take you on a battlefield outing for years. They have your name. They have mine. What makes me think I can ignore this very real possibility? It has happened before.

Arnold's father was drafted for both WWII and Korea. This may have caused him to be more fearful of being recalled. He often told me he could not go again. I told him we would leave the country if that happened. He seemed unsure of this solution. During our time at the University of Oregon in Eugene we attended protest marches. It was all we could do to show our support for ending the Vietnam War and saving lives including Arnold's.

Impact Statement

I was in Vietnam. The trauma I experienced is associated and ignited by a few powerful people who ostensibly wanted to stop the spread of communism. It was a mistake to think the armed forces of the U.S. could render useless a determined guerrilla force.

My involvement was a matter of chance, being of the right age at a time when the draft was used to bring the military to a certain strength.

My reaction was probably similar to others who had the same exposure. I saw mayhem on the ground and and saw bombardment on a large scale from the air. The images of death and use of huge amounts of ordinance, the sounds and smells stay in my mind and remain out of scale with any other thing that resembles normal life.

I remain vigilant because some mistakes may be made by others in power in our world. Today is peaceful, and I feel safe. I will not automatically trust everyone because I've seen how power and control can affect me and change my life. My self esteem is not high because "I fell for it." I allowed the draft to take me, and I killed people. My feelings are intact and are guarded.

I have always believed Arnold could not relate to a 19 year old teen being put in this situation. He saw himself as an adult, but he wasn't. He was still a kid, and of course he could be brainwashed by the military to shoot and kill. I always wished his therapist would have brought that up to him.

The therapy I have received from the VA has helped. I have more understanding about PTSD and have learned about how I have affected others in my life.

Again therapy was just a reminder of the guilt he felt about how he retreated from and rejected his family and friends. How was that good therapy?

We talked about our feelings and how we were put away (with no escape) from most of our duty tour. This would often happen when we got a new man "a greenhorn". Their fear seemed strange and somewhat humorous. But, we all admitted we were just like them when we first arrived and had we remained consumed by fear, we wouldn't have done much work, everywhere in the 1st Marine Division's territory. What could we do about danger? We couldn't avoid it, so all that we could do was to be extremely prepared.

In the beginning, our operations were formally organized action plans with some goal. We were well versed in just how the Marine Commanders could use our services. For example, the Commanders would often want to use us tactically by setting us up on the right flank to broadcast disturbing sounds, like sirens and screeching. Sure it is disturbing to the NVA and VC, but then they came for us and at the speakers, with mortars, rifle fire or a VC squad were sent to take us out. We did not want to be in the field drawing fire. We had to do something to avoid this situation. Avoiding certain fire fights kept us safe at times. This became our tactic (avoiding fire fights) as time went by.

We did some civic action working with the Civic Action Patrols which were located in small compounds right in the fire zones. *They might see the need for some villages and hamlets to get some food or supplies. We could obtain those items and take them out on our next trip. Care was taken to not over supply these people because often they were forced to turn over their rice for the NVA cause. If the Marines felt the NVA were close by, they would burn the bags of rice.*

Our Psyop's team had various programs that were constantly employed. One program was the the surrender or Chieu Hoi program I talked about earlier. The government of South Vietnam offered amnesty to VC, and Chieu Hoi included a safe life in Saigon and schooling for a trade. To surrender, we instructed the NVA to hold up a bright yellow coupon or a Chieu Hoi ball, which we dropped daily in the rural areas and areas of current fighting. When we got a Chieu Hoi surrender, our interpreter would interrogate him, and we would take photos. The surrendering soldier was asked to say something to his comrades such as how good his care was. Then we would write a leaflet, specific to his unit, and drop these within days. This of course happened if the surrendering VC soldier was not killed by U.S. soldiers, which happened often. "Target practice" they would say.

Bomb damage was more visible from the air. I flew as a spotter in a small airplane (O2B) several times dropping leaflets. What I saw was shocking. The sight of damage caused by the war was unbelievable. The terrain in I Corps (northern most province) was pockmarked from bombs. There were craters everywhere.

Having a love of nature, this upset Arnold terribly. Nature was sacred to him.

My impressions at the time was that the bomb coverage was very widespread. I heard the bombs all the time. At night rolling thunder operations were used against the NVA and their supply routes. B-52s cruise at a very high altitude, out of sight and sound and the 500 pound bombs exploded in the distance in a steady rain. The sight of all the beautiful terrain, destroyed in little hundred mile radius wells reminded me of the serious possibility of being in a spot that could become a crater.

Arnold was with Marines on occasion in North Vietnam fighting. He never knew if U.S. aircraft knew where the Army and Marine squads were. That caused tremendous fear most likely for all the soldiers.

My Attitude and Philosophy

The treatment for my PTSD by the VA over the last couple of years has involved detailing stressful events and trying to determine why these intrusive thoughts are coming to me. I have discovered that many, many of the incidents that I see as intrusive are just general thoughts sights, smells and sounds, and they never leave. Because our days were often spent dealing with situations that most people would consider their stressful incident, I had so many that the term stressful incident seems laughable. Everyday was stressful. Everyday was traumatic.

One big influence in my life, 44 years since returning from the war, is the mindset and attitude that came by soon after my worst incidences. I mentioned that we were in danger all the time. Actually, it seemed as though I was ignoring danger. I was not careless or going unprepared by no means, but my death might come at any minute. I didn't know when or where, so why worry or even think about it. Others in my unit felt similarly.

I worked daily in a war and to be effective, we had to use some pretty wild rationalizations that may have made a permanent change in me. I will try to describe my mindset.

I was and am still hyper vigilant, studying all people to detect signs of trouble. Therefore I am prepared to meet any situation by use of maneuvers, planning and weapons. I still do this after all these years. As in the rocket belt area, a person could not easily see who was friendly and who would kill you at first chance. Other Marine divisions in I Corps would shoot anything that moved. We could not do that. I saw Vietnamese men age 12-50 who would likely be a member of what ever government had the advantage at the time. We just did not know who was VC or NVA.

At one point, early in my tour, I changed a lot. During a rocket attack, I took a concussion from a rocket that landed very close to me. The take away point was that I was in real danger. It was a kind of awakening. We were being exposed to injury and death, and unplanned actions. There was no discussion of the incidences as being sensational. We did not explain any incidences to the other men, except to warn of danger and make suggestions about how to improve our operation. Otherwise, we just tried to forget it and bury it deep within our minds.

U.S. troops did not always show respect to the Vietnamese people. I saw how the "use" of the young Vietnamese girls affected the feelings of her family and village. They took it in stride. They had seen it all their lives with the French, Chinese and the Americans. Our team suffered untold hardship due to the actions and *attitudes of some soldiers. I felt vulnerable because I would be associated with the crude behavior of these soldiers.*

Arnold told me that young village men would prostitute their teenage sisters. One American dollar for sex. Arnold had sex with a teen girl once. He says all he remembers of the young woman was her staring up into the blue sky, maybe trying to escape in her mind what was happening to her. His action left him saddened and with feelings of guilt.

Trauma in Vietnam

Shortly after arriving in Vietnam and on my way to the 1st Marine Division, rockets hit near the runway of the Da Nang airbase. I remember three rockets coming in about five seconds apart. I was with a group of five guys. Immediately, after the first explosion, I stopped and ran to the other side of where I was. I jumped into a trench when another sharp blast hit us. This scene damaged me forever.

My head felt odd. I had a concussion. I felt as though I'd been hit with a fist, but without any specific point of pain, and I seemed stunned. I looked across the runway and scanned for more trouble. I was seeing with new eyes. Everything was crystal clear, bright and colorful in contrast to how I was seeing before Vietnam. My sense of smell was peaked, and I smelled familiar scents with a new intensity, the dust, the fuel and oil products and some Vietnamese domestic smells of food from a nearby refugee camp. This new way of being would never leave me.

Fire Fights

Fire fights and snipper action were a constant problem every-where in our operation area. While driving, we would hear shots, some of which hit our truck and were always present in our atten-tion. We usually kept on rolling at high speed but on occasion we would stop and take up a defensive position. This was frustrating because all would end, and we were left wondering if there were more snipers and how large the enemy unit was.

The strategy of the NVA and VC was to harass us with random sniper fire. One or two VC could fire then more and five again in a couple of hours. Just two guys following us out of a 60,000 man enemy. A patrol of ten or more VC could lead to a chase, thinking we had contacted a large enemy unit. Suicide sappers were a con-tinual threat and was a strategy used by the NVA Sapper Division to lead an attack on an installation or military base. The thought of a group of men sneaking up and giving their lives to breach a wire or blow up ammo storage areas was eerie and very hard to understand. I was using survival techniques to stay alive but understood how survival moved to slow the advancement of our patrols and and units. When we fully understood that we may die at anytime, hesitation or second thoughts were no longer a factor.

Power of Ammo

Suicide Sappers slipped into the munitions storage bunkers close to the airport, that was sheltered somewhat by Hill 327. I was at Headquarters when the ammo started exploding. This hap-pened in my first days outside Da Nang. A rain of debris with occasional live bombs, kept up for over two days. We were essentially grounded and under cover. The explosions were large, and the concussion flattened our regional PX, also the Freedom Hill PX and totally flattened the refugee camp. This occurred on the outskirts of the the Da Nang airport. The refugee village known as Dog Patch, was constructed of found materials; sheet metal, cardboard and wood and was extremely dense, with a small alley as a way to come and go out of the village. The entire area was destroyed, flattened to the ground.

Today Dog Patch has been rebuilt and exists much as it did in 1968.

The Liberty Bridge on the DMZ

The road used to travel to the 5th Marines at Hoi An was essential for use by a large Marine force. After trouble with the bridge, the Marines stationed a platoon permanently there, about three miles from the Regimental Head Quarters. We figured this was under control. However, the bridge was completely blown up in the spring of 1968. "I was there when it happened." Arnold wrote.

He and his troops were actually in North Vietnam. There was no way back, except by air. Arnold said he was never so scared. He was sure he would be captured or killed. They were later rescued by helicopters. Arnold said this further reinforced his feelings of vulnerability. He never talked about why the Marines and Army were in North Vietnam. I would presume they were chasing the NVA.

Malaria

Malaria was a continuing problem, and we took a weekly dose of quinine to prevent it. Mosquitos were everywhere, and I was continually bitten. One of my men refused to take his medicine because it made him sick. I tried to figure out how the pill could be taken with less ill effect. Taking this medicine with food did not help. Although he was a good soldier, he was ill all the time. Within six months he was finally shipped off after reporting to the China Beach Medical Hospital.

This seemed unbelievable that we have bullets and bombs and fire to survive, and if we do, we still have a chance of being taken out of action by a mosquito!

My Stuck Points

I can't believe I can improve.
Trusting people is dangerous.
My happiness has been crippled. I'm hollow. I'm dead.
I'm hyper vigilant all the time.
I just don't care.
I need to be prepared.
I need to check every situation.
I will always be a shooter.
I will always be a killer.

My Challenge Answers

I am a shooter ready and able to kill humans.
This will never change.
Evidence: I've done it. It is based on facts.
Situations result in action (in war).
After war, unlikely, but real.

My information is reliable. At home in the world, the probability is likely lower than I think it is.

My feelings are based on fact. They are not irrelevant.
I'm not exaggerating.
Trusting is dangerous. I've done it.
Have met people I trusted.
I've had experience with men who are not trustworthy.
I'm talking about the loss of life. My information is reliable.

Low probability in the U.S, but absolutely possible.
I witnessed things that were beyond any doubt.
What I talk about is fact.
My happiness is crippled.
I feel hollow inside, no emotion. I feel empty and flat.
I've felt it everyday for 47 years.

I feel cold blooded. I take risks without questioning someone else's safety or welfare.

Interpretation follows action from encounters in Vietnam.
I'm a shooter, and the decision will be made quickly.
My information is reliable.
When I am vigilant there may be only a small probability of a confrontation.

Inner Control Sources (How I cope)

Food and drugs (alcohol, marijuana, cocaine, speed in my 20s and 30s). I now rely on hydrocodone, tobacco, and marijuana to relieve my pain and anxiety. I just can't sooth myself. I have inner emptiness and deadness. I am excessively self criticizing and am always overly cautious.

My Take Away

I've lost self respect being under control of the 1st Marine Division and being told what to do regardless of my moral objections.

Trust is a ticket to death. I have lost trust of any person or organization including our government. I'm angry at people who actively avoided the draft. I'm hyper vigilant. I need to be in control. I will never get better.

My happiness is crippled. I have thoughts of death and destruction on a daily basis.

Hyper vigilance is absolutely necessary. Enemy and civilian people were everywhere in our territory because the Da Nang Air Base was the source of stupendously deadly weapons. It was the largest tactical airbase in the world. The mission of the 1st Marine Division and my Army Division and Psyop teams was to protect the airbase and the city.

Chapter 19

WISE NOTES TAKEN
DURING PSYCH SESSIONS

While cleaning out files in Arnold's studio I found some writings about philosophy. I never knew he was interested in this topic. But, I have found many pages detailing what he had read and how he thought about the topics. I found additional notes in Arnold's journal. These are the works that he could relate to and wrote about.

Spinoza notes

Emotion, which is suffering, ceases to be suffering as soon as we form a clear and precise picture of it.

Nietzsche notes

He who has a why to live for can bear almost any how. But why aim for life, when a strong person has to bear the terrible how of their existence.

It does not really matter what we expect from life, but rather what life expects from us. Stop thinking about the meaning of life, but rather what it expects from us. Stop asking about the meaning of life, and instead think of ourselves as those who are being questioned by life daily and hourly. Our answers must consist, not in talk and meditation, but in straight action and right conduct. Life ultimately means taking the responsibility to find the right answer to its problems and to fulfill the tasks which it constantly sets for each individual.

Notes about my spirit

My spirit is the non physical part of me. It is the seat of my emotions and character. In the Army I lost my soul. I no longer belong anywhere. The Army molded me into the person I will be for the rest of my life. My spirit is broken.

My good qualities: I have courage. I'm brave, and I have energy, determination and assertiveness. I use systematic reasoning. I have self discipline. I set goals. I'm hard working. I have perseverance and I can problem solve. I'm patient.

However, I am immodest. I lack humility and decency. I'm improper and indelicate. I'm bold, brazen, immoral, impudent, shameless, loose and wanton. As a teenager I was feisty, gutsy, ballsy. I had strong determination. I was outspoken and streetwise as a teenager. I remained this way all through my adulthood. I wish I had dignity and pride and a sense of self worth.

Many days I am in physical and mental anguish. I'm quick to anger. I am defiant and some times despicable. I never take orders from anyone. In war, I was hostile and aggressive. I can be cross and annoyed. I am spirited, ornery, and stubborn. I am defiant and can be unruly.

All of these things I saw in Arnold at times, but during "the good years", his negative qualities were balanced out by all the good he had inside him. To me he was a good, kind, and a very smart man. He was driven by work and play. He brought me comfort, pleasure and always made me feel safe. Our marriage was easy after I understood how PTSD affected him. He was not a bad person. He just thought he was.

Things I need to learn

I need to learn poise, feel a sense of assurance, and grace. I need to feel self confident again. I need these pleasing qualities. I must see beauty in my manner, motion and action. I need to set goals and work hard. I must persevere.

I don't understand etiquette for my social behavior within society. I need to phrase statements in a non-confrontational manner.

This is something I saw at times. Arnold did not understand etiquette, and he would occasionally say something inappropriate to family and friends and co-workers. But, people understood his demons and seemed to forgive him for these outbursts.

The chaotic modern world – Arnold's thoughts about life in the world today

Life requires flexibility, adaptability and a mind set to be able to change.

We need to bend without breaking. Be ready and able to change. Flexibility applies to whatever can be bent without breaking whether or not it returns to its original shape. Being inflexible made me aggressive, combative, belligerent, confrontational and always ready for a fight.

Adaptability is a very important attribute a soldier must have.

We must be able to adjust to new conditions, be able to modify ourselves for a new use or purpose.

What is Mindset

It is the established set of attitudes held by someone. It is a settled way of thinking or feeling about someone or something. Attitude is reflected in a person's behavior. I am very competitive, and that is the attitude of my mind. I am also resentful and antagonistic. I wish I could change.

My attitude is a settled way of thinking or feeling about something or someone. Our attitude is reflected in a person's behavior. It is a good thing to be competent in your attitude. It is the position of your body. For me, I am resentful and antagonistic in manner. I also never understood etiquette or living within norms. There were times that I would have to remind Arnold that he was being rude. It made him feel bad, but it never produced a different outcome. You could be rude to your buddies and think nothing of it. I guess that was the norm in the military. It did not work well in regular society. Other than working with clients, Arnold had little contact with our family and friends towards the end of his life. Throughout his career, I often attended client meetings with Arnold to help him keep calm.

Arnold then begins talking about the war in Afghanistan.

Arnold said, *"We need to end this culture of impurity."*

When the Iraq war started, Arnold, Steve and Allan talked a lot about the uselessness of this war, a repeat of Vietnam. All were extremely upset, but in time they seemed to accept it and did not speak of the new war much. They knew they could do nothing about it.

Chapter 20

PTSD HOMEWORK ASSIGNMENTS FROM PTSD COUNSELING, 2012

It appeared that Arnold had regular weekly homework assignments, but completed very few of them. His first assignment was to talk about the election of George W. Bush. All he wrote was that he was at 100% stressed out. He no longer talked as much about war and became a little more focused on our future lives.

He worried about money and his current lack of work. This never bothered me as I still worked at our local hospital and made a good living. Arnold had social security, disability payments, and a small pension. Arnold's work was different as a self employed architect. On one hand, he either had no work and no pay, or he had a lot of work and made very good money. Our house and cars were paid off, so the worry about money, I couldn't understand. He reported that finances put him at a 50% stress level. He may have thought it was his duty to provide for me. I had told him from our first date, "I can take care of myself, and it is important to me that I can do that." My father had instilled this virtue into me at an early age. Not going to college was not an option. My Dad wanted the best for me, and for me to have the confidence of a woman who knew what she wanted and could get it. Though my parents gave me a great deal of freedom, I fully understood their expectations of me. I hoped this would ease Arnold's mind, but evidently it didn't.

Arnold wrote that we liked to travel. We both liked to hike and did this activity up until four years before he had his strokes. Both his back, feet and knees began bothering him, and he was in pain much of the time. Later, in the hospital, I would find out that Arnold had nine ruptured disks. Doctors could not believe he could walk. Yet, he continued outdoor activities. When we were able to go hiking and camping he said his stress level was a zero. He loved the outdoors. He loved nature and the feeling of peace it gave him. I do believe that being bed bound after the strokes left him with terrible fear and a feeling of not being able to escape to the mountains and deserts he loved so much.

Arnold had a gun and a knife by his bedside at all times. We tried one trip after he was paralyzed going to the desert in eastern Oregon. It was not a success. He refused to get out of the hotel bed. Our friends Steve and Sheri came with us and having Steve there was some comfort for me, as Sheri and I could go for walks and go swimming, but for Arnold it provided nothing. He never tried to get into his wheelchair during the days of our trip.

Arnold wrote that in the year 2009, we took in my cousin Brittany. She had been in jail on a drug charge. We thought living a normal life with us would help her with her life. She had been in foster care during her teen years and had experienced abuse as a child. She was 19 when she came to live with us. Arnold felt he was seeing no improvement in Brittany's life. She still, occasionally did meth. When with her at home, Arnold had low anxiety. In social situations with Brittany, he said he was at a 60% stress level. Shopping with Brittany was extremely difficult, but he did it because she liked to do this activity with Arnold. Black Friday was her favorite shopping day. When she had her child Andrew, Arnold's stress level became less noticeable. He loved that little boy. Today, Arnold would be proud of Brittany and her husband, as they have made a good life for themselves and their four children.

Frightening memories return

During one week of therapy he actually did document his moods of intrusive memories. He wrote "INCOMING" over and over and said this meant, mortar, artillery, rockets and firepower all coming towards him and his squad. He was back in Vietnam.

These notes were taken in January of 2012. He wrote daily for 14 days. His first thoughts were of active swarms of memories, stirred strongly during his psych session (AMBUSH/INCOM-ING). I'm extremely fearful.

The second day he had problems sleeping, with more active memories in his dreams.

The third day he had intermittent flashes, a somber mood, feelings of depression. He had 14 hours of flashbacks and little sleep.

The next day he had low scale visualizations and five hours of flashbacks. He also had thoughts of his friend Tom and someone named Bob and went to other scenes of war. Total hours of flashbacks for this day were four hours and six hours the next day.

The later days his flashbacks were mild, but constant. He had a total of 18 hours of flashbacks.

The next days were consumed with thoughts of Vietnamese civilians and explosions.

The last days dealt with his time with Brittany. He says he was 60% distressed when he took her shopping at the mall. He could not go into some of the stores as there were not enough windows for him to feel safe. He could not see what was going on.

Comments from Arnold's documentation

My thoughts include images and sounds from war and seem to be constant. All time is thought of in the context of war. Intrusive thoughts happen often, sometimes a repeated scenario. It is difficult to remember times of duration.

Arnold would tell me that his 19 months in Vietnam were a blur. He could not recall what happened (activities, fire fights and people) in terms when they occurred.

Today's session stirred my memories, like a rake through the coals stirring up blowing embers, bright, loud and perfectly detailed.

As Arnold prepared to come home, he began to think of a normal life. He and his friend Allan would talk about the girls back home. They wanted to marry soon after returning. They wanted a woman who was kind, honest, and most importantly trust worthy, oh and pretty too! Arnold thought about marrying an Asian girl, as he thought no American girl would be interested in being with a Vietnam vet. But, they married American girls who would love them, regardless of Arnold and Allan having to continue to live with the horrors of war. Living with PTSD is something many military wives live with daily. All we have to offer is love, comfort, and understanding. I don't believe there is a cure for PTSD. It engrains itself their minds, never to leave. Oh, how wished I could have helped Arnold somehow, but war memories seldom left him.

PART 4

Chapter 21

THE END

Arnold's last four years of life were very difficult. He kept only to himself and spent most of his time outdoors and traveling in his truck. I never knew where he would go for hours on end. He wanted little contact with me. There were times when I wanted to shake him. I didn't want him to leave me. We had a lot of time left to love and laugh, to move on to new adventures and to chase new possibilities.

I began pushing him to get help, but he would not. On May 17th, 2015 he went into heart failure. He was at the Portland VA and the Puget Sound VA for more than 10 months. During that time he had four strokes and became paralyzed.

We were home for a year, where his mental and physical state continued to worsen. When he began to lose the use of his hands, he gave up. He chose to die by not eating and not drinking fluids. It took him 27 days to die. We told no one. And, I kept hoping he would change his mind, as although he was very ill, he was stable and his medications kept him that way. But, a bladder infection would spread and his kidneys quit functioning. It took him two days to make his final exit from this life. He was in terrible pain and would not allow me to call an ambulance. I think he wanted to die in pain just as many of his fellow soldiers had. He called out to them often that last day. It seemed to me that he did not want to die peacefully, and he no longer wanted to be put on life support: However, that is what happened when we got to the hospital. He was still in terrible pain and finally the hospital sedated him for the last six hours of his life. Even sedated he still did not seem peaceful as his body and eyes were twitching. Was he trying to escape something, maybe life. I don't know. What I do know is that he went boldly to war and he went boldly to his death.

Funeral Eulogy

Arnold, the man I loved and knew was a soldier and a warrior. He was also a man that for 47 years suffered from anger, guilt, sadness, insecurity, and loneliness.

Arnold was drafted into the Army in 1967. He served two combat tours, 19 months in Vietnam as a psychological operations squad leader. He was with the first Marine Division, where there was heavy fighting on the DMZ. 14,000 men would die in his combat division.

Arnold did and saw things in Vietnam that he could not endure, or come to terms with. He felt he was damaged and evil. He felt that people he met saw that in him.

In reality, what we all saw was his brokenness but also love, understanding, warmth and kindness.

Arnold, I know today that those painful thoughts for you are gone forever. And I know that you are truly resting in peace. You have crossed to the other side of the wall.

Epilogue

The plane begins a slow decent into the Da Nang Airport. I put my hands up to my face and begin to sob. I have waited 48 years to come here to experience Vietnam, to walk where Arnold walked, to smell the air, to feel the heat, see the people and hear an unfamiliar language.

I always felt Arnold and I had so much in common. We grew up in blue collar families. We went to college together. We married young. In many ways, we grew up together. What was missing for me was the 19 months he spent in the Vietnam war. I had asked Arnold many times in our later marriage if we could go to Da Nang. His answer was always "no". Arnold's war buddies were also not keen for me to go. What would my reaction be, sadness or feelings of peace? I was willing to take the chance. I needed to connect the war stories with the actual place. Also, since Arnold died, I ask myself everyday, where is your soul? Did you go back to Vietnam? Would I find him there?

As I was standing in the customs line in Da Nang a four or five year old Vietnamese girl smiled at me. She was beautiful. Was she the reincarnation of the child Arnold killed? I could not take my eyes off her. She felt so familiar.

My Godson Ed came with me on the trip. It was a joy to have him with me. He is more adventuresome than I am, and we went more places and did more things on our own. We got good at taking the local train to other cities. And, Ed got to see some places his Dad was at in 1969.

I was so excited to be in Da Nang. The first day I wanted to go to Freedom Hill and the first Marine Division headquarters. Most people I talked to said there would be nothing there to see, but there was.

We took a taxi past Dog Patch which looked much the same as the pictures I had seen from 1968, vendors selling trinkets, and then we arrived at the Gate of Freedom Hill. There were two guards there. I showed them a picture of Arnold and they bowed to me and told me to look around and stay as long as I wanted. My boots were on the ground that Arnold walked on many times. There was not much there. On the top of the hill is a rock quarry, so no hootches to see. However, there was an old French guard house, a rusted tank, and two concrete bunkers. I took in a deep breath of the hot air and picked up a handful of warm red earth and let it sift through my hand. I listened to the cicadas in the trees, I did not feel his presence at all the whole time I was in Vietnam.

Freedom hill 2019

The following day, we went to a small war museum. There was an old man at the door to collect donations. I showed him the picture of Arnold. He bowed and shook my hand, and then said "I was a soldier too." The museum had a room dedicated to Ho Chi Minh. I have since become more interested in this man who spent his life trying to unite his country. Outside there were a few planes, tanks and trucks the U.S. had left behind. Everything was rusting and decaying. The war is truly over. American soldiers are revered as they were doing what they thought was right. I met a few both north and south Vietnamese people who said they wished the Americans had stayed, and they could be a democracy. I realized they understood democracy better than I thought.

Later in the week we visited Marble Mountain and Monkey Mountain. Both were beautiful places with beautiful statues of Buddha and Hindu Goddesses places Arnold and Allan could only see from the top of Freedom Hill. I was told there were Marine units at the bottom of the mountains and yet inside the tunnels there were NVA hospitals. Soldiers so close to each other physically, yet so far away in their beliefs.

We spent a day in Hoi An, a 2000 year old city, known as the city of lanterns. We went on a boat ride and lit prayer candles to place in the water. I prayed for Arnold to stay close to me. It was a beautiful sight at night.

We also went to the Hue, the forbidden city, and the Citadel (college). This is where the last Vietnamese emperor lived in seclusion until 1932. The architecture was very ornate and beautiful. All had been restored since TET. Arnold would have loved to see that.

Near the end of our trip, we spent four days with a north Vietnamese college student. She hired a driver for us to visit North Vietnam. We toured a local kindergarten school and a library funded by U.S. soldiers (Children's International Libraries) and built by local craftsmen, a true collaborative effort between the U.S. and Vietnam.

After the visits, we headed farther north. We saw three small statues of Vietnamese soldiers at the DMZ, nothing grandiose. We traveled the Ho Chi Minh trail, now a very nicely paved highway. We saw the new Library bridge, still a walking bridge. The north painted blue and the south painted yellow with both flags flying from the middle, representing reunification.

Trinh, Author and Ed

We had dinner at our student's home and toured the family farm. No more straw huts. Villages look much like farms in the U.S. with brick, marble, and concrete homes, very nice. Our student offered to show us the VC tunnels on her grandparents farm, but we declined to look.

As we spent our last days in Da Nang I came to feel that this country has healed itself. There is a Buddhist vibe to the country. People are kind and loving, open to meeting all visitors to their country. They always bow and shake your hand when you meet someone new. They honor all soldiers. It was fate that brought Americans to Vietnam. There is no anger, just new friendships to be made.

As we boarded the plane to come home, I felt I had come to do what I needed to do. I knew the Vietnam war of 1968. Now, I knew it in peace in 2019. And, I know now that Arnold's soul is not there. He remains in my heart. Both of us can move on, me in the physical world, him in the spirit world, hopefully to be united again one day.